'HOW TO'

BOOK OF SALADS AND SUMMER DISHES

JACQUI HINE

D1829210

BLANDFORD PRESS
POOLE, DORSET

The 'How To' Book of Salads and Summer Dishes explains in straightforward terms, through the use of concise texts, tables, photographs and diagrams, the methods of making a range of salads, dressings and garnishes that will suit every taste and occasion.

'HOW TO'

Contents

The 'How To' Book of Salads and Summer Dishes
was conceived, edited and designed
by Simon Jennings and Company Limited,
42 Maiden Lane, London WC2, England

General Editor: Michael Bowers
Art Direction: Simon Jennings
Text: Jacqui Hine
Illustrations: Lindsay Blow
Photography: John Couzins, Peter Higgins Peter Mackertich
Design and Research Assistant: Caroline Courtney

First published in the United Kingdom 1982

Link House, West Street, Poole,
Dorset BH15 1LL, England

ISBN 0 7137 1055 1
Printed in Singapore

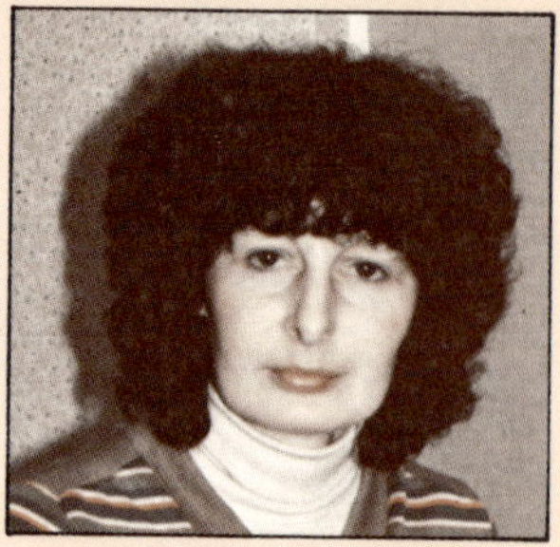

THE AUTHOR

Jacqui Hine gained her teaching diploma in Home Economics at Seaford College and taught for 5 years. After a year in Switzerland sampling the cosmopolitan cuisine, she returned to London and became Home Economist for the British Farm Produce Council where she was responsible for the recipes used in the Telephone Recipe Service. For the past 3 years Jacqui has been a cookery journalist with the popular monthly magazine, Family Circle.

Introduction

"Banish the 'rabbit food' syndrome for ever!" Nearly all edible plants can be used in salads, giving a wide variety of flavours, colours and textures all year round.

Salad dressings can be as exciting. Some can be made in seconds, others take a little longer, but once you've mastered the technique of a silky, home-made mayonnaise you'll always find those few extra minutes to make it. Different flavourings can be added to the dressings to vary the salads even more. The choice is yours. Don't feel embarrassed when serving a one-vegetable salad, the French do it and consider it a course in its own right. If you've a little more time, mix several vegetables together; James II is said to have enjoyed over 32 different ingredients in his salads! If you like to enjoy the flavour of each individual vegetable serve them in separate bowls or in small heaps on the plate. The Spanish serve their salads this way as *hors d'oeuvres.*

For a special occasion, why not follow the American style of presentation and make a moulded salad? And if you can't get used to serving cold salads in winter, serve it hot as they do in Germany. For those who find it difficult to chew raw vegetables, a liquid salad makes a refreshing drink which is also good as a starter to a meal.

The choice is limitless and in the following pages you'll find advice on buying and preparing vegetables and making them into simple or mixed salads for every occasion. Be creative, visit your greengrocer regularly and try new vegetables. The advice in this book mainly concerns vegetables bought loose; if you buy them from the supermarket they are often cleaned and trimmed, and you may find they don't keep so well.

Most of the recipes are for 4 persons but this is meant only as a guide, because it will depend on how and when you serve them. In most cases it will be easy to halve the quantities if you only want sufficient for two. If you get into the habit of serving salads regularly, not only will you be providing tasty and exciting menus, but extra goodness that is often lost in a dish of cooked vegetables.

What are salads made of?

A salad is a dish of one or more vegetables, either cooked or raw, coated in a well-seasoned dressing. Although a salad may include other ingredients such as meat, cheese and eggs, it is the preparation, arrangement and dressing of the vegetables which make it a salad. There are very few vegetables or fruits which do not appear, at some time, in a salad recipe. This gives you the opportunity to buy only produce which is in season. Consequently, your salads will always be fresh, crisp, full of flavour – and economical.

Salad produce
The best way to choose your salad ingredients is to go to a market such as the one shown *left*. Almost every town and city in the world has its equivalent of the street market. For centuries, people have been able to examine the produce at close quarters and argue about the price. This is a service that your supermarket cannot provide. Salads, of course, do not consist entirely of vegetables. Fruit, *above*, and dairy produce, *top*, form an important part of many of the recipes in this book.

Salads through the ages

From the beginning

Man has always relied on plants for a substantial part of his diet. All the plants we know today, and many others, originally grew wild and earliest man would pluck roots, leaves, flowers and seeds from them as he passed. He had no way of knowing which parts of the plants were edible, and while some nourished, stimulated or healed him, others poisoned him. When the Northern ice caps receded and Europe became a temperate forest region, man settled down in small camps and his eating habits became more regulated. While the men hunted animals, the women gathered wild roots, leaves and fungi and developed basic cooking techniques.

The vegetables we know today are undoubtedly the edible plants most frequently gathered by these women. Seeds dropped near the camps would have flourished and become the first 'cultivated' vegetables.

The Romans

The Romans introduced numerous varieties of vegetables throughout their empire and handed on the techniques of cultivation and making kitchen gardens. Salads or 'vinegar diets' were popular because they were economical, requiring no cooking, and satisfied the appetite – making it unnecessary to serve bread or other accompaniments. No wonder, when the salads consisted of over a dozen varieties of vegetables mixed with as many different herbs. The whole was laced with a strong vinegar dressing, the forerunner of our more delicate oil and vinegar dressings.

After the Romans

After the decline of the Roman Empire, interest in vegetable growing diminished and, in Europe, only the monks continued to grow their own vegetables. Wild plants and herbs continued to be used, and during the Medieval period a salad might have consisted of twenty or more varieties of herbs, each carefully selected for flavour and colour. Flowers were used as garnishes. Vegetables continued to decline in popularity over the next few centuries, and while the wealthy piled their tables high with meats and fish, the poor had to survive on the few vegetables they could grow or pick. Although many plants and herbs were surrounded by myths, many continued to be used and by the mid-16th Century, salads had become an important part of a meal, often served with hard-boiled eggs.

A new gastronomic era

The 17th Century saw European cooking emerging as a fine art. Vegetables, although still referred to as herbs, were now classified. Vegetables for cooking were called 'Pot Herbs', those that could be eaten raw were referred to as 'Sallet Herbs' while those used only for flavour were known as 'Sweet Herbs'. The first cookery books appeared at about this time and included recipes for 'Simple Sallets' using green leaves, oil, vinegar and sweet herbs. Other recipes for 'Mixed Sallets' or 'Salmagundy', consisted of almonds, raisins, oranges, lemons, sage, cauliflower, cabbage, lettuce, currants, dates, oil and vinegar. Meat or fish were often included.

Salad dressings became more elaborate and were thickened with the yolks of hard-boiled eggs for mixed salads. Simple salads or side salads were served with oil, vinegar and sugar dressing or with vinegar only.

Although agriculture rapidly increased during the 17th Century and glass houses were constructed, they were mainly for tropical fruits and decorative vegetables. It was not until the 18th Century that some of the myths surrounding vegetables were exploded. Salads became simpler, herbs were omitted and meat or eggs arranged on a bed of shredded lettuce, beetroot, radishes, chicory and celery became common. The salad would be covered in a creamy-textured dressing made with milk or cream.

The adverse effect of a high protein diet was beginning to be recognised, and vegetables once more increased in popularity. By the end of the century there were numerous market gardens flourishing on the outskirts of most large towns and their produce was readily sold to both the wealthy and the poor inhabitants of the towns.

The modern salad

During the last few decades the salad has been sadly abused. Tomato and lettuce on the plate has become the accepted norm served with cream dressing from a bottle. Recently, however, because of extensive travel and a renewed interest in wholesome foods and dietary control, the salad is once more gaining in popularity and providing us with an opportunity of blending flavours, textures, colours and extra nutrients into our diet.

Salad dressings

Everybody would agree that a salad is incomplete without a dressing; some would say that the dressing makes the salad. The job of the dressing is to perform a complementary rôle – bringing out the flavours of the salad ingredients and contributing its own. Traditionally, mixed vegetable salads should have either an oil and vinegar dressing *(vinaigrette)* or a thickened egg dressing *(mayonnaise)*.

1 Salt and pepper
Vital to almost every dressing
2 Garlic oil
Made with mild oil: *recipe page 37*
3 Herb vineger
Use wine vinegar: *recipe page 36*
4 Herb oil
Again, use mild oil: *recipe page 36*
5 Vinaigrette
Use wine or cider vinegar: *see page 38*
6 French dressing
The classic salad dressing; use good quality olive oil: *see page 37*

7 Olive oil
Buy the best you can afford
8 Tomato dressing
Good with all green salads: *see page 43*
9 Mayonnaise
Another classic dressing: *see page 38*
10 Oil and vinegar
Basic ingredients of many dressings
11 Garlic dressings
A good dressing for bean salads: *recipe page 45*

Storing ingredients
Oil and vinegars for dressings should be kept in securely stoppered containers. The glass jars with cork stoppers shown here are ideal.

Salads and nutrition

"Make food your medicine and medicine your food".
From the doctrine of Hypocrates.

Vegetables and fruit

These are an important part of our daily diet, and should be included in every meal. Ideally, 50% of our daily intake of vegetables should be raw. They are nutritionally important because they provide us with:

Vitamins, especially *Vitamin C,* which are necessary for general health and vitality, *Vitamin B* for the release of energy from the foods we eat, and *carotene* which is converted by the body to *Vitamin A* for clear skin and good vision in the dark.

Mineral salts, especially *iron* to enrich the blood, and *calcium* for strong bones and teeth and good clotting of the blood.

Fibre which, although not digested by man, acts as bulk to the faeces and aids the removal of poisonous waste products from the body. Fibre can be found in the skin and fibrous structure of all fruit and vegetables.

Water which is essential to life and aids bodily functions. Two-thirds of our body weight is water and it is present in the blood and every cell in our body. 80% – 90% of vegetables and fruit is water.

Proteins for building and repairing our body cells, found mainly in edible seeds such as beans, peas, nuts and also in potatoes.

Starch, which is stored in the roots, tubers and seeds by most plants – providing us with a useful source of energy. But because a smaller quantity of raw vegetables can be consumed at one meal than cooked vegetables, the salad makes an ideal dish for those on a calorie-controlled diet.

Loss of Nutrients

The important vitamins and mineral salts described above are easily lost or destroyed by careless handling, storing, preparing and cooking of the vegetables.

Advantages of eating raw vegetables

The principal advantage of raw vegetables is that far fewer nutrients are lost compared to cooked vegetables. Additionally, the fibrous content helps the passage of unwanted matter through the body and raw vegetables are, of course, less fattening. They may also provide a greater variety of texture, flavour and colour.

COMPOSITION OF SOME POPULAR SALAD INGREDIENTS

Per 100 grammes (3.5 ozs) of edible material	Waste percent	Energy K/cal	Energy KJ	Protein g	Fat g	Carbohydrate g	Calcium mg	Iron mg	Carotene *(Vit A)* Mg	Thiamin mg	Riboflavin mg	Nicotinic Acid mg	Vitamin C mg	Vitamin D Mg	Water percent
Beetroot *(raw)*	18	28	118	1.3	trace	6.0	25	0.4	–	0.03	0.05	0.1	6	–	87.1
Beetroot *(cooked)*	20	44	189	1.8	trace	9.9	30	0.4	–	0.02	0.04	0.1	5	–	82.7
Cabbage *(white/green)*	–	22	93	1.9	trace	3.8	44	0.4	trace	0.06	0.05	0.3	40	–	90.3
Cabbage *(red, raw)*	30	20	85	1.7	trace	3.5	53	0.6	*(20)*	0.06	0.05	0.3	55	–	89.7
Carrots *(maincrop)*	4	23	98	0.7	trace	5.4	48	0.6	2000	0.06	0.05	0.6	6	–	89.9
Cauliflower	30	13	56	1.9	trace	1.5	21	0.5	30	0.10	0.10	0.6	60	–	92.7
Celeriac *(boiled)*	21	14	59	1.6	trace	2.0	47	0.8	–	0.04	0.04	0.5	4	–	90.2
Celery	27	8	36	0.9	trace	1.3	52	0.6	–	0.03	0.03	0.3	7	–	93.5
Chicory	21	9	38	0.8	trace	1.5	18	0.7	trace	0.05	0.05	0.5	4	–	96.2
Cucumber	23	10	43	0.6	0.1	1.8	23	0.3	–	0.04	0.04	0.2	8	–	96.4
Endive	37	11	47	1.8	trace	1.0	44	2.8	2000	0.06	0.10	0.4	12	–	93.7
Lettuce	30	12	51	1.0	0.4	1.2	23	0.9	1000	0.07	0.03	0.3	15	–	95.9
Mushrooms	25	13	53	1.8	0.6	–	3	1.0	–	0.10	0.40	4.0	3	–	91.5
Mustard & Cress	–	10	47	1.6	trace	0.9	66	1.0	*(500)*	–	–	–	40	–	92.5
Onions	3	23	99	0.9	trace	5.2	31	0.3	–	0.03	0.03	0.2	10	–	92.8
Peppers *(green)*	14	15	65	0.9	0.4	2.2	9	0.4	200	0.08	0.03	0.7	100	–	93.5
Potatoes *(boiled)*	14	80	343	1.4	0.1	19.7	4	0.3	–	0.08	0.03	0.8	*(4-14)*	–	80.5
Radishes	50	15	62	1.0	trace	2.8	44	1.9	trace	0.04	0.02	0.2	25	–	93.3
Tomatoes	–	14	60	0.9	trace	2.8	13	0.4	600	0.06	0.04	0.7	20	–	93.4
Watercress	23	14	61	2.9	trace	0.7	220	1.6	3000	0.10	0.10	1.6	60	–	91.1
Apples	23	46	196	0.3	trace	11.9	4	0.3	30	0.04	0.02	0.1	3	–	84.3
Grapefruit	52	22	95	0.6	trace	5.3	17	0.3	–	0.05	0.02	0.2	40	–	90.7
Oranges	25	35	150	0.8	trace	8.5	41	0.3	50	0.10	0.03	0.2	50	–	86.1
French dressing/Basic	–	658	2706	0.1	73.0	0.2	5	0.1	–	–	–	–	–	–	23.5
Mayonnaise/Basic	–	718	2952	1.8	78.9	0.1	16	0.7	trace	0.06	0.11	trace	–	1.0	23.0

NB. Approximate values only – taken as raw except where stated. 1 milligram = 1,000 micrograms (Mg)
1 gram = 1,000 milligrams *(mg)*

Salad starter dishes

Salads make perfect starters because they are able to stimulate the appetite with subtle, but distinctive, flavours without being too bulky and filling. A great many salads can be adapted to become starters, but those shown on this page are specifically intended as appetisers. Starters should be quite small portions and individually served, although crudités may be generally distributed around the table.

Yoghurt dressing
Yoghurt is much underrated as a basis for dressings, but it is perfect for a sauce to serve with crudités: *recipe page 41*

Avocado boat
Avocados are a safe choice; this is an interesting variation: *recipe page 52*

Crudités
When served as strips, raw vegetables can be dipped into a sauce before eating: *recipe page 47*

Pear and crab starter
Use firm, fresh pears when possible for this unusual and subtly flavoured dish: *recipe page 51*

Prawn cocktail
This is probably the best known of all starters, but no less delicious for that: *recipe page 50*

Tomato and celery cups
It is not easy to make this dish look so tempting as it does here, but it is well worth the extra effort: *recipe page 48*

Salad making equipment

Equipment
There are only a few basic pieces of equipment necessary to prepare good salads. You will find those described here more than adequate for the salads in this book.

Knives
Good stainless steel knives can be sharpened. Ordinary steel knives have a better cutting edge but tend to discolour when used on certain vegetables and fruit. For basic preparation you will need three: a small 8cm (3in) blade for peeling, a 23cm (9in) blade for slicing and chopping, and a small serrated knife for paring.

Chopping board
This is essential for all slicing and chopping. Keep one side for strong smelling foods and use the reverse side for fruit, etc.

Potato peeler
Ensures that only a thin layer of peel is removed – thus preserving essential vitamins.

Grater
A 4-sided grater is best because it stands firmly on the board.

Pestle and mortar
Useful for pounding garlic, nuts and herbs. Avoid wooden types because they absorb smells and flavours.

Salad basket
Necessary for shaking leafy vegetables dry without bruising the leaves.

Scrubbing brush
A small bristle or vegetable brush is useful for cleaning roots and stalks.

Food processor
Useful if large quantities are to be prepared. Most models have separate blades for chopping, slicing, shredding and grating. They can be electric or hand operated.

Refrigerator
Most have a salad compartment at the bottom. Do not keep salad ingredients in a very cold refrigerator.

Salad bowl
This should be wooden. They are available in a wide range of styles and sizes. Never wash a wooden bowl, just wipe with a damp cloth. Each time before using, season the inside of the bowl with a little salad oil and rub round a cut piece of garlic or onion.

EQUIPMENT FOR MAKING SALADS

- Knives
- Chopping board
- Potato peeler
- Grater
- Pestle and mortar
- Salad basket
- Scrubbing brush
- Food processor
- Salad bowl

OTHER USEFUL ITEMS

- Muslin
- Kitchen paper towel
- Damp cloth – *either linen or muslin kept specially for wiping fruit and vegetables*
- Garlic press
- Egg slicer
- Lemon squeezer
- Parsley chopper

EQUIPMENT FOR DRESSINGS

Balloon Whisk
Essential for mayonnaise. Choose a small one that's easy to manage.

Basin
Should be deep-sided to allow ingredients to be beaten without splashing.

Salads as side dishes

Side salads are served as accompaniments to main dishes, usually when the main dish is strongly flavoured or spicy. The salad should be chosen to offset the flavour of the main dish rather than to compete or clash with it. Side salads are essentially simple, usually consisting of no more than two vegetables. A variety of dressings may be used, but simple oil and vinegar kinds are the most usual.

Sweet pepper and tomato salad
One of the most versatile of side salads: *recipe page 59*

Coleslaw
This is an ideal winter salad and is at its best with cold or spiced meats: *recipe page 61*

Watercress & orange salad
An ideal dish to serve with rich food: *recipe page 55*

Minted beetroot bowl
A colourful salad to serve with cold meats: *recipe page 56*

Broad bean & caraway bowl
The combination of young broad beans and caraway seeds gives an unusual and delicate flavour: *recipe page 57*

Courgette & tomato salad
In this salad the courgettes are cooked a little to bring out their flavour: *recipe page 57*

SOME SUITABLE SALAD VEGETABLES

On the next few pages, we deal with the choosing and preparation of the vegetables which form the basis of this book.

Preparing salad vegetables

DON'T ●	BECAUSE ●	DO ●
Buy more vegetables than you need	Prolonged storage causes loss of flavour, nutrients and crispness	Buy them as fresh and as often as possible
Leave vegetables in a warm room	Light and heat accelerate deterioration and loss of vitamins	Store correctly in a cool, dry, dark place
Leave vegetables soaking in water	Vitamins B and C will be absorbed into the water	Prepare just before using. Wipe with a damp cloth, swish through a bowl of cold water or rinse under gently running cold water
Pat leafy vegetables dry in a cloth	This bruises the leaves and releases vital juices	Swing dry in a salad basket or place in a large piece of muslin, gather up corners and swing vigorously out of doors.
Peel unless necessary	a) Valuable nutrients are just below the skin b) Skin adds colour and texture to salad c) Provides extra roughage	Wipe with a damp cloth
Cut leafy salad plants unless shredding	Valuable juices are released and some Vitamin C is destroyed	Tear leaves. Break off stalks whenever possible
Prepare leafy salads in advance	Leaves become flabby and tough when mixed with a dressing	Mix root and stalk vegetables. Toss leaves in at last moment

VEGETABLE	CHOOSING	STORING	PREPARING
Beetroot *All year round. New beets start in June.* 	**Uncooked:** Baby beets are sold in bunches, larger ones loose. Look for firm fresh beets with bright, unbroken skins. **Cooked:** Buy freshly cooked ones with skins that rub off easily. They should be firm and a rich red in colour.	**Uncooked:** Do not trim. Store in a cool, dark, airy place and avoid breaking the skins. **Cooked:** Place in a dish, cover and store in the refrigerator up to 3 or 4 days. For longer storage, cover beetroot in vinegar.	**Uncooked:** Peel and grate coarsely. **Cooked:** Peel and leave baby beets whole. Larger ones can be sliced or chopped.
Cabbage ***White Cabbage:*** *October to February* ***Red Cabbage:*** *August to January* 	The best cabbage is heavy for its size. Large heads are now sold in halves or quarters. Choose firm, compact heads and avoid those with limp, curling or blemished leaves.	Wrap cut cabbage in cling film and store in refrigerator. Store whole cabbages in a cool, dark airy place.	Strip off damaged or wilted leaves and trim stem. Cut head in half from top to stem, then each half into quarters. Shred cabbage by cutting across leaves into very fine strips.
Chinese Cabbage *November to June.* 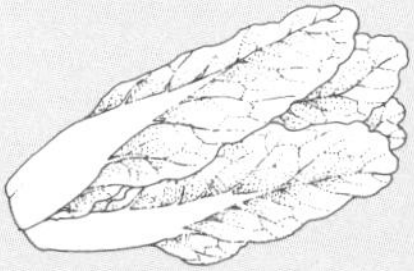	Sold by weight and should be heavy for its size. Choose one with fresh, crisp stalks and leaves. Avoid wilted ones.	Store in a plastic bag in the refrigerator. Long term storage is not practicable.	Cut thin slices across cabbage starting at the leafy end *or* separate leaves and strip off fleshy parts from stalk. Finely chop stalk and pull leaves into bite-sized pieces.
Carrots *All year round. Young carrots June to August.* 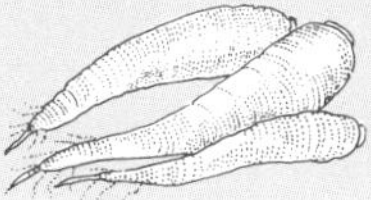	Young carrots are sold in bunches with foliage. They should be no thicker than your thumb. Choose firm, bright-orange and smooth-skinned ones.	Do not trim or wash until ready to use. Store in a cool, dark, airy place.	Do not peel or scrape baby carrots. Gently scrub in cold water, trim off tops and use them as garnish for salads. Use baby carrots whole or thinly sliced. Larger carrots can be coarsely grated.

See pages 24-25

Salads as main meals

A well-balanced salad can be perfectly adequate as a main meal. The inclusion of cheese, meat or eggs will give the salad a substantial protein content and, when served with rice or boiled potatoes, it will lack nothing in nutrition, texture or flavour.

Continental bean salad *right*
This is a rich and substantial salad that easily makes a meal. Can be served with garlic dressing or French dressing: *recipe page 68*

Carrot and date salad
A good salad for picnics and one that does not suffer in transit. Try it with a cheese and onion dressing: *recipe page 67*

Chicken salad *left*
Almost a tradition now, for summer lunches or al fresco meals. Serve with mayonnaise: *recipe page 74*

Tomato & bean shoot salad
This salad is served well chilled and is delicious in hot weather. Serve it with a tomato dressing: *recipe page 73*

VEGETABLE	CHOOSING	STORING	PREPARING
Celery *Most of the year.* 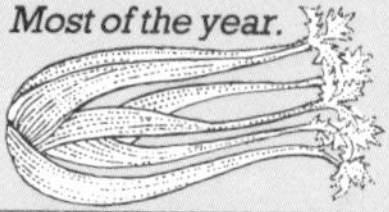	Celery should be firm and crisp. A few green leaves should be attached. Avoid soft, bruised stalks.	Store in the refrigerator. If limp, stand stalks in ice-cold water to crispen.	Pull away stalks from base. Scrub stalks in cold water with a small brush. Chop crunchy base for salads and use leaves for garnish.
Celeriac *Mainly during the winter months.* 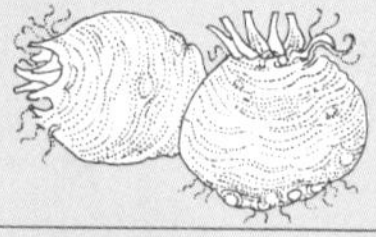	Look for firm, undamaged roots that have no sign of rooting. Roots larger than an orange could be hollow or woody.	Can be stored for some time in a cool, airy place.	Cut off thick, tough woody skin and cut root into quarters. Thinly slice or grate quarters. To prevent discolouration, mix immediately in vinegar or salad dressing.
Chicory *Most of the year, especially winter months.* 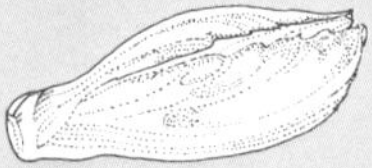	Chicons should be crisp, white and fleshy. Avoid those with brown marks on the leaves.	Store in the refrigerator.	Pull off any damaged leaves and wipe chicon with a damp cloth. Either separate leaves or cut across chicon into thick slices. Use at once as cut surfaces discolour.
Courgette *Most of the year.* 	The best courgettes are no fatter than a fat cigar, or longer than 10cm (4in). Choose firm, dark green ones, avoiding those that are soft and wrinkled.	Store in a cool, dark place or in the refrigerator.	Wipe with a damp cloth, then trim both ends. Either slice thickly or chop by cutting into four lengthwise and slicing each quarter thickly.
Cress *All year.* 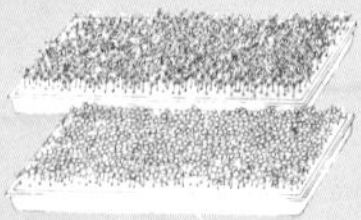	Can be grown at home or bought while still growing in little punnets. Choose only bright, healthy cress.	Keep in a cool place, dampening peat if necessary. If stalks are allowed to grow too long the cress will lose its flavour.	With a pair of scissors, snip off stalks to within ½cm (¼in) of base. Place cress in a sieve, rinse in cold water and shake dry in a piece of muslin. Use at once.

VEGETABLE	CHOOSING	STORING	PREPARING
Cucumbers *All year round, especially late summer.* 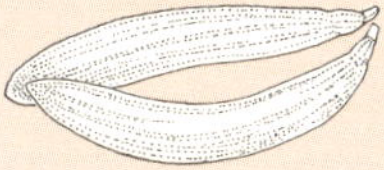	Pick firm, dark-green cucumbers that are no thicker than 5cm (2in). Avoid soft ones, especially at stalk end.	Store in refrigerator or in glass of water stem-end down.	Cut off quantity required and wipe skin with a damp cloth. Slice or dice by cutting into four lengthwise and slicing each quarter thickly.
Dandelion Leaves *All year but best in Spring.*	Cultivated dandelions can be blanched in the garden to make them less bitter. Choose young leaves and strip them from the plant by hand.	Use immediately after picking.	Wash leaves in cold water and shake dry in a salad basket. Use with lettuce or other green salad plants.
Endive *Autumn and Winter but often scarce.* 	The curly leaves should be yellowy-green in colour, firm and dry. Dark green leaves will be bitter.	Store in the refrigerator.	Pull off any outer damaged leaves, trim off root base, separate stalks and break into small sprigs with a little stalk on each. Wash and leave a few minutes to crispen in ice cold water, then shake dry in a salad basket.
Fennel *(Florence)* *Florence fennel is available all year, especially late Summer and Autumn.*	Choose well-rounded roots, pale green to white in colour. Avoid dark green, yellow or soft ones.	Keep in a cool, dark airy place or in refrigerator.	Wipe with a damp cloth. Trim root base and cut root in half lengthwise. Cut thin slices across each half starting at stalk end.
Herbs Traditionally, salads were made with numerous varieties of herbs and we should not neglect their use in today's salad.	Use fresh herbs if possible, and as soon after picking as possible. **N.B.** If only dried herbs are available, use less than half the quantity stated for fresh herbs.	Herbs can be stored for indefinite periods after drying, but will best preserve their aroma, colour and flavour if kept in lightproof, airtight containers.	Leafy herbs such as parsley, mint and sage can be washed, stripped from the stalk, and patted dry. Roughly chop or crush the leaves so that the juices can escape

See pages 28-29

Hot salads and others

It is important to remember that salads cover a very wide range of possibilities. They are not merely arrangements of mixed raw vegetables. Hot salads, of which ratatouille is a classic example, are usually substantial enough to be main course salads. Moulded salads may require a little more preparation time than others, but they are ideal for parties or occasions which call for especially attractive presentation. Liquid salads are extremely nutritious and convenient – they can provide the benefits of a meal in a quick and refreshing drink.

Ratatouille salad
Served either hot or cold ratatouille makes a substantial dish: *recipe page 81*

Hot kebab salad
Delicious when served hot and crisp on a bed of rice. Serve with a soured cream dressing: *recipe page 82*

Mixed vegetable mould
This attractive dish is usually served as a side salad: *recipe page 87*

Melon boats
These make impressive starters, but they are quite easy to make: *recipe page 86*

Cucumber cool
A delightful drink; refreshing, with a pleasant tang: *recipe page 92*

Carrot & Celery cup
Packed with nutrition, a meal in itself: *recipe page 93*

Apple & orange refresher
A delicate mixture of sweet and sour flavours: *recipe page 92*

Tomato and celery cup
This has a big, spicy flavour and makes a substantial snack: *recipe page 93*

VEGETABLE	CHOOSING	STORING	PREPARING
Lettuce *Most of the year, especially summer.* 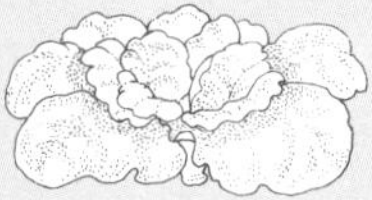	There are many different varieties but all should be firm, well-developed and full-hearted. Avoid wilted or slimy lettuces. If outer leaves have been removed, this could indicate that the lettuce is not fresh.	Use as soon after picking as possible. Otherwise store in the refrigerator.	Cut off root and remove any damaged outer leaves. Separate leaves by tearing, never cut. Wash each leaf separately under gently running cold water. Shake dry in a salad basket.
Onions *Large onions all year. Salad or spring onions scarce in winter months.* 	**Large onions** are sold loose and should be firm with dry, brittle skin. **Salad onions** are sold in bunches with green stalks still attached. Choose small, firm bulbs. Avoid any onion that is soft and mushy.	**Large onions** should be stored in a cool dry, airy place. **Salad onions** can be wrapped to avoid flavouring other foods and stored in the refrigerator.	**Large onions** Peel off dry skin and either slice from stalk end or chop finely. Grate against the grain to make onion juice. **Salad onions** Snip off ends of stalk only and trim roots. Peel off thin outer skin and slice down through centre of stalk and bulb, if large.
Garlic *All year round* 	Buy one bulb at a time as each clove is very strong. Choose fresh, firm, dry, plump bulbs with dry papery skins for the best flavour.	Store in a cool, dry, airy place.	Peel off sufficient papery skin to expose one clove only. Remove clove with the thumbs and avoid damaging rest of bulb. Peel clove and chop finely or crush in a garlic press.
Mushroom *All year round – wild ones late Summer.* 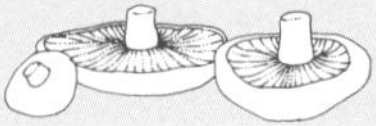	Mushrooms are sold in 3 stages of maturity: **Button** - tightly closed **Cup** - half open **Flats** - fully open Look for firm white caps with fleshy stems.	Use as fresh as possible. Exposure to air, once picked, turns them flabby. Exclude all air by placing them in a tightly closed bag in the refrigerator.	Never wash or peel mushrooms. Wipe with a damp cloth and trim away dirty base of stalk. Use whole or sliced, raw or cooked.

VEGETABLE	CHOOSING	STORING	PREPARING
Sweet peppers (*Capsicums, Pimentoes*) *Available most of the year.* 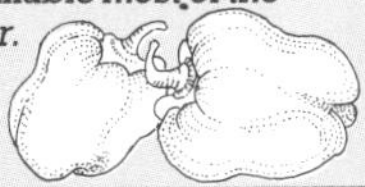	As the fruit ripens, it turns from deep green to deep red in colour and becomes sweeter in flavour. Choose firm, shiny peppers, avoiding soft or wrinkled ones.	They keep well in the refrigerator. Wrap cut ones in foil.	Wipe peppers with a damp cloth and cut in half lengthwise. Remove stalk, seeds and white pith. Either chop, slice thinly or cut into strips down length.
Radishes *All year, especially in Summer.* 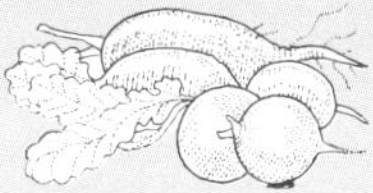	Salad radishes are usually sold in bunches with leaves attached. The radishes can be red or white, round or tapering. Choose hard, medium-sized ones, avoiding those that are spongy.	Store radishes in a plastic bag in refrigerator.	Trim off roots and stalks completely. Wash radishes and use whole or thinly sliced.
Tomatoes *All year, but plentiful in Summer.* 	For salads, choose firm, medium-sized tomatoes with a matt skin. Deep red ones are usually over ripe.	Place tomatoes carefully in a bowl and store in refrigerator, any soft ones can then be easily seen and removed.	Remove calyx and wipe tomato with a damp cloth. Slice, or chop tomatoes by cutting into 4 or 6 wedges and cutting across each wedge.
Watercress *All year, but sometimes scarce.* 	It is not advisable to pick wild watercress. Cultivated watercress sold in bunches should be bright green and very fresh looking. Avoid yellow leaves and thick stalks.	Remove any yellow leaves and place bunch of watercress in a jug of cold water. Cover with a plastic bag and store in the refrigerator. Best eaten within 24 hours of purchase.	Discard yellow leaves and any stalk that is thick or long. Leave other stalks on. Rinse watercress in cold water and shake dry in a salad basket. Break into smaller pieces, if necessary. Use on its own or with another green salad plant.

Garnishes

A garnish is not merely a piece of decoration on top of a dish. It should considerably enhance the salad by adding a little touch of flavour and texture – as well as colour. Often, when a salad is served with a sauce, the garnish will be one of the ingredients of the sauce. Vegetables and fruit are the usual material for garnishes although, as you can see here, other ingredients such as eggs and bread (croutons) may be used. Vegetables should always be very fresh and very crisp.

For making garnishes see page 32

GARNISHES
from left to right

● TOP ROW
Lemon wedges
Useful for squeezing a little juice over dish
Lemon Butterflies
Good for decorating many dishes
Lemon twist
Ideal decoration for cups and long drinks
Julien strips
The best way to prepare crudités.

● CENTRE ROW
Tomato waterlily
Tricky to prepare but decorative.
Egg wheels
Easy to make and can be used on many salads
Celery tassels
Ideal to use with dips and sauces
Gherkin fan
Attractive and easy to prepare.

● BOTTOM ROW
Radish rose
A popular garnish for a wide range of salads
Cucumber wheels
Easy to make and popular with children
Croutons
Delicious with soups as well as salads
Tomato roses
Not so pretty, but just as good as waterlilies

Preparing garnishes

WEDGES

Use lemons, oranges or tomatoes. Cut the fruit into quarters from the top to the stalk end. Slice each quarter lengthwise into 2 or 3 wedges. To perch on a rim of glass, make an incision through the white pith from one end.

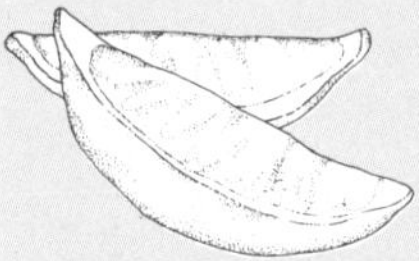

BUTTERFLIES

Use lemons, oranges, tomatoes or cucumber. Thinly slice fruit across the width. Cut each slice in half and make a cut almost to the centre of each half. Pull the quarters round to form a butterfly shape.

TWISTS

Use lemon, orange, tomato or cucumber. Thinly slice the fruit across width. Make one cut to the centre on each slice and twist the pieces either side of the cut in opposite directions.

JULIENNE STRIPS

Root Vegetables: Peel, if necessary, and cut a thin strip from one side so that the vegetable lies flat. Thinly slice, place 2 or 3 slices on top of each other and cut into thin strips.
Cucumber, courgette, etc.: Wipe and cut into quarters lengthwise. Cut each quarter into 2 or 3 strips, again lengthwise, and cut strips into 7cm (3in) lengths.

CELERY TASSELS

Wash and cut a stick of celery into 5 cm (2 in) lengths. Cut along the length of the stick at narrow intervals almost to the base. Alternatively, cut from both ends almost to the centre. Place celery in ice-cold water until ends curl.

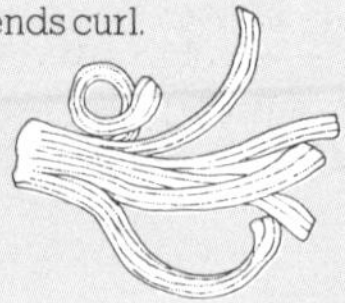

GHERKIN FANS

Cut each gherkin, lengthwise, into 4 or 5 slices almost to the stalk end. Spread out slices to form a fan.

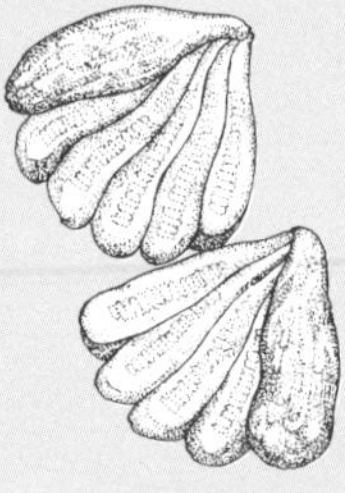

RADISH ROSES

Small round radishes make the best roses. Trim, wash and make 4 cuts through the radishes almost to the stalk end. Place the radishes in ice-cold water until they open out like a rose.

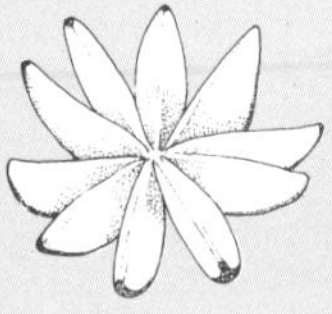

CUCUMBER WHEELS

Wipe the pieces of cucumber and score down the length with a fork all the way round before thinly slicing. For a bolder effect, remove alternate strips of peel.

TOMATO WATERLILY

Use firm tomatoes and a small, sharp-pointed knife. Wipe the tomato and cut round it in small 'v' shapes, inserting the knife to the centre of the tomato each time. Carefully twist and pull the two halves apart.

EGG WHEELS

Heat a little oil in a small omelet pan. Beat an egg, pour into pan and cook over a low heat until set but not browned. Slide the omelet onto a plate, roll up tightly and leave until cold. Cut the roll into thin slices.

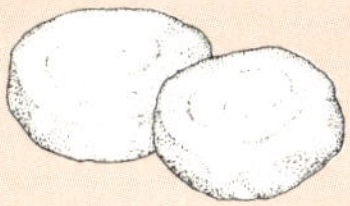

CROÛTONS

Cut day-old bread into 5mm (¼in) thick slices, trim crusts and cut the bread into cubes. Heat a little oil or butter in a pan and fry the cubes until golden brown on all sides. Drain on kitchen paper and use cold. A little crushed garlic may be added to the butter or oil.

TOMATO ROSES

Use small, firm tomatoes and a small, sharp or serrated knife. Thinly cut the peel from the tomato in a spiral and re-curl the skin to form a rose shape.

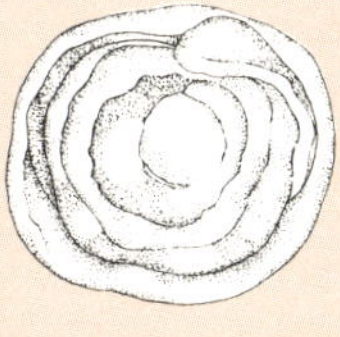

Metric measurements

The metric and Imperial measurements used in these recipes are approximate only. Quantities of vegetables bought by weight are calculated to the nearest kilogram or pound.

Metric spoons are useful for measuring oil, vinegar, salt and other ingredients. Sets of metric spoons are available from most hardware stores although some makes do not include all four sizes.

Equivalent measures	
15ml spoon	= 1 level tablespoon approx.
10ml spoon	= 1 level dessertspoon approx.
5ml spoon	= 1 level teaspoon approx.
2.5ml spoon	= ½ level teaspoon approx.

If no 2.5ml spoon is available for measuring dry ingredients, use a deep teaspoon, level it off with the back of a knife, and divide the spoon as shown.

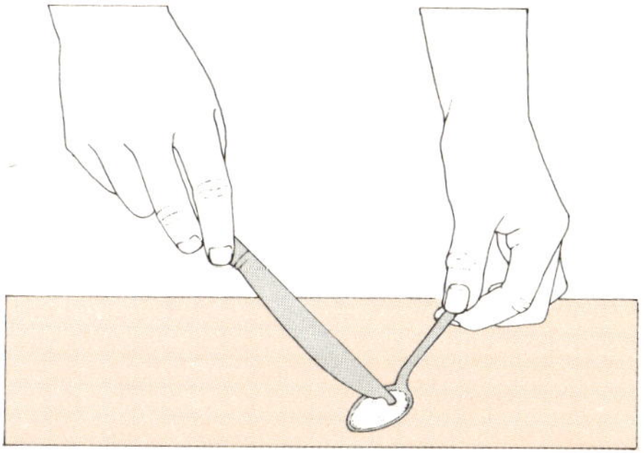

SALAD DRESSINGS

Mixing salad plants with a dressing is a very old custom, probably begun by the Romans who poured a harsh vinegar over their salads, oil being difficult to obtain.

Types of dressing

A dressing not only adds extra flavour and moisture to a salad but helps to provide the dish with extra nutrients. Most salad dressings derive from three basic types: **A:** oil and vinegar dressings, e.g. French dressing, **B:** thickened egg dressings, e.g. Mayonnaise, **C:** Dairy dressings, e.g. Yoghurt, soured cream or evaporated milk dressing.

●

French dressings and Vinaigrette

These are used mainly with simple salads consisting of one or two vegetables or leafy salad plants.

Proportions

Use 2 to 3 parts oil to 1 part vinegar or lemon juice. A little salt and pepper is added, and often a pinch of sugar to tone down the acidity and a pinch of mustard which helps to bind the oil and vinegar together.

Method

Place all the ingredients in a bottle with a plastic or plastic-coated screw-top. Shake the bottle vigorously until contents are well blended.

Storage

The dressing will keep some time, but the oil and vinegar will separate out again. Simply reshake before using. Other flavours or ingredients can be added to the basic dressing (*see page 38*).

Mayonnaise

This is the most widely used form of salad dressing. Commercially made salad creams are available, but most have strong flavours which tend to dominate the salad.

Proportions

Approximately 125ml (¼ pint) oil is used to each egg yolk, 15ml (1 tablespoon) vinegar and a little seasoning.

Method

It will take 15- 20 minutes to make a perfect mayonnaise by hand. The oil has to be added drop by drop to prevent the mixture separating. Large quantities can be made in a liquidiser or food processor and the oil added slowly through the top.

Storage

Home-made mayonnaise will keep several weeks if placed in a container with a tightly fitting lid (not metal) and stored in a cool place. It may begin to separate if kept in a very cold refrigerator and certainly will if placed in the freezer.

Dairy dressings

Yoghurt makes an excellent salad dressing, not only because it's easy to use, but also because it is a useful ingredient for the diet conscious. Soured cream, canned cream and cream cheese also make good dressings.

INGREDIENTS FOR DRESSINGS

"A salad is only as good as its dressing, and a dressing is only as good as its ingredients".

An old saying that's just as true today as it was several centuries ago.

Oil

The choice of oil is important. Choose a good quality salad, sunflower or safflower oil. Avoid using an ordinary vegetable cooking oil as the flavour is less refined. If you are using an olive oil, choose the best you can afford. Olive oil is an acquired taste so it's a good idea to buy small quantities until you find one to suit you. The addition of oil to a dressing provides extra vitamins and acts as a lubricant to the digestive system.

Vinegar

Use a wine, cider or herb vinegar (see page 36). Never use a malt vinegar which is harsh and used mainly for preserving. Lemon juice makes a good stubstitute when a milder dressing is required.

Egg Yolks

Use large fresh eggs at room temperature. Ingredients used straight from the refrigerator are likely to separate.

Herb vinegars & oils

Herb vinegars can be purchased, but are very simple to make if you grow your own herbs. Herb oils are made in the same way.

Ingredients/equipment

Herbs Use fresh herbs such as mint, tarragon, marjoram or chervil. The herbs should be picked in early summer or at least before they flower.

Vinegars Use wine or cider vinegar. Malt vinegar is too strong.

Oil Use a bland-flavoured oil such as a good quality sunflower or safflower oil. A mild-flavoured olive oil may also be used.

Bottles Choose a wide-necked bottle with a plastic or plastic-coated screw top. Vinegar will quickly discolour a metal top.

Method

1 Gather the herbs when they are dry and pull the leaves from the stalks. Bruise the leaves between the hands as this will help to release their flavour.

2 Place sufficient bruised leaves into a wide-necked jar to loosely fill it.

3 Cover the leaves with vinegar or oil, screw on the top and leave the herbs to infuse 2 weeks. (If making herb oil, place the bottle in a warm place, but not in direct heat, or the herbs will begin to cook.)

4 Strain the vinegar or oil through a fine sieve, pressing the leaves to extract all the juice. Pour the vinegar or oil back into a clean bottle and place a fresh sprig of the herb in the vinegar bottle. Cover the bottle and label.

N.B. *If the vinegar or oil is not sufficiently flavoured, repeat the process with more bruised leaves.*

"It takes four to make a dressing
A spendthrift to pour the oil
A miser to add the vinegar
An accountant to add the salt
And a madman to stir."

An old American saying.

Garlic oil

2

This is very strong, so remember to use only a few drops at a time and make in small quantities.

●
Ingredients

Garlic Use only very fresh bulbs with firm, fat cloves

Oil Use any mild-flavoured, inexpensive salad oil.

●
Method

1 Peel and roughly chop garlic cloves. Lightly crush them with a round-ended knife or use a mortar and pestle.
2 Pack in sufficient crushed garlic to two-thirds fill a small bottle. One large garlic bulb should be sufficient to flavour 125 ml (¼ pint) oil.
3 Cover the garlic with oil and leave the bottle in a warm place, away from direct heat and sun, for 2 to 3 weeks, shaking daily.
4 Keep the garlic covered by replacing the oil as it is used. Renew garlic after 2 to 3 months.

●
N.B. *When peeling and crushing garlic, work in a well-ventilated room to prevent odours lingering.*

French dressing

3

This classic dressing is always made with a good quality olive oil.

●
Ingredients

Olive oil	2 × 15ml spoons (2 tablesp.)
Wine vinegar	1 × 15ml spoon (1 tablespoon)
Salt	½ × 2.5ml spoon (¼ teaspoon)
Black pepper	a good grind

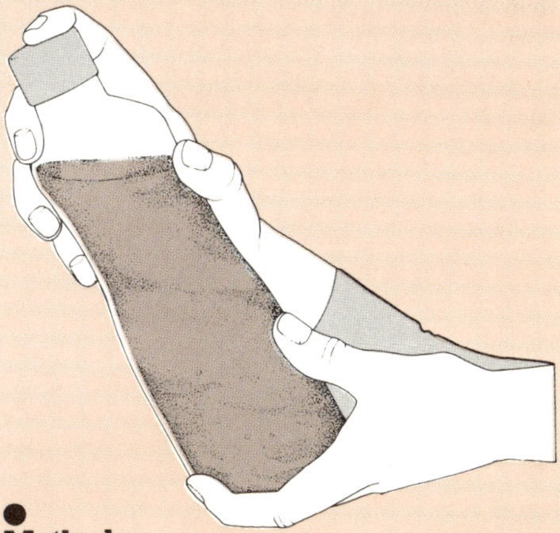

●
Method

Place all ingredients in a bottle with a plastic or plastic-coated screw-top. Shake the bottle vigorously until the contents are well blended. Use at once or re-shake before use.

Vinaigrette 4

Any type of salad oil may be used with wine, cider or herb vinegar. Other ingredients can be added to the basic recipe.

●
Ingredients

Oil	2 × 15ml spoons (2 tablesp.)
Vinegar	1 × 15ml spoon (1 tablespoon)
Salt	½ × 2.5ml spoon (¼ teaspoon)
Dry mustard	½ × 2.5ml spoon (¼ teaspoon)
Sugar	½ × 2.5ml spoon (¼ teaspoon)
Black pepper	a good grind

●
Method

Place all ingredients in a bottle with a plastic or plastic-coated screw-top. Shake the bottle vigorously until the contents are well blended. Use at once or re-shake before use.

Variations

Add any of the following to the basic recipe:

A a few drops of Worcestershire sauce
B a few drops of soy sauce
C finely chopped capers or gherkins
D finely chopped onion
E finely chopped or crushed garlic clove
F freshly chopped herbs

Mayonnaise 5

Make sure all the ingredients are at room temperature. To help you add the oil slowly, place the measured quantity in a small-necked bottle fitted with a cork from which a small section has been cut. Mayonnaise can take up to 20 minutes to make, but it should be a very satisfying process. It is very important not to rush through it.

●
Ingredients

Egg yolk	from one large egg
Salt	½ × 2.5ml spoon (¼ teaspoon)
Dry mustard	½ × 2.5ml spoon (¼ teaspoon)
Pepper	½ × 2.5ml spoon (¼ teaspoon)
Sugar	a pinch
Salad oil	approx. 125ml (¼ pint)
Wine vinegar	1 × 15ml spoon (1 tablespoon)

●
Method

1 Place egg yolk, salt, mustard, pepper and sugar in a bowl. Whisk with a small balloon whisk until thick.

2 Add oil, drop by drop, whisking well between each addition. When one-third of the oil has been absorbed, the rest may be added a little more quickly. The mixture should be very thick at this stage, but you may add a few drops of the vinegar if it is too stiff to whisk.

3 When sufficient oil has been added to make a thick creamy consistency, slowly

whisk-in the vinegar. The finished mayonnaise should be smooth, glossy and the consistency of thick cream. Taste, and add more seasoning, if required.

N.B. *A little warm water may be added if a thinner consistency is preferred.*

WHAT WENT WRONG?

If the mayonnaise curdles and separates instead of thickening, it could be caused by one of the following reasons:

1 The ingredients were too cold
2 The egg yolk was stale
3 The oil was added too quickly

To Save a Separated Mixture

First, whisk a teaspoon of hot water into the mayonnaise **or,** whisk 1 tablespoon of the separated mayonnaise in a clean bowl with 1 teaspoon each of hot water and vinegar, then slowly whisk in the separated mixture. If these methods fail, then you will need to use another egg yolk to save it. Whisk an egg yolk in a clean bowl and then slowly whisk in the separated mixture. The finished mayonnaise may be thicker, so whisk-in a little extra oil and vinegar until the required consistency is reached.

Alternative mayonnaise

Mayonnaise by machine

Most liquidisers and food processors won't make less than a 2-yolk quantity successfully. The recipe is the same except that the vinegar is placed in the machine with the yolks and seasoning *before* the oil is added, instead of at the end. Follow the manufacturer's instructions.

Whole Egg Mayonnaise

For a lighter, creamier mayonnaise use the whole egg, instead of only the yolk, and add more oil. (This mayonnaise can only be made by machine.)

Additional flavourings

Gently fold any one of the following into the mayonnaise just before using: single cream, mustard, chutney, grated lemon or orange rind, tomato ketchup.

Family mayonnaise (boiled)

Although sharper and less rich in flavour than the traditional mayonnaise, this boiled dressing is often more acceptable to younger members of the family who seem so fond of the commercially-produced salad cream. For an even milder flavour, use a greater proportion of water to vinegar. The mayonnaise stores well in a bottle with a screw top either in the refrigerator or in a cool cupboard for several weeks.

●

Ingredients	
Plain flour	3 × 15ml spoons (3 tablesp.)
Sugar	1 × 15ml spoon (1 tablespoon)
Dry mustard	1 × 5ml spoon (1 teaspoon)
Salt	1 × 5ml spoon (1 teaspoon)
Pepper	½ × 2.5ml spoon (¼ teaspoon)
Egg	1 standard
Water	125ml (¼ pint)
Wine vinegar	125ml (¼ pint)
Salad oil	*see method*

●

Method

1. Place flour, sugar, mustard, salt and pepper in a saucepan and mix to a paste with the egg.
2. Gradually stir in the water, then the vinegar.
3. Cook over a very low heat, whisking continuously, until the mixture thickens.
4. Continue cooking over the low heat for a further 5 minutes, stirring occasionally.
5. Pour mixture into a bowl and whisk occasionally until it's almost cold.
6. Gradually add sufficient oil to make a thick coating consistency, about 6 x 15ml spoons (6 tablespoons).
7. When cold, pour mayonnaise into a bottle, cover and store in a cool place.

Tip *Don't cook the dressing too quickly or it may curdle or become lumpy. If you can't stir the mixture continuously, place it in a basin and stand that in a pan of gently boiling water.*

Yoghurt dressing 8

Ingredients

Natural yoghurt, or soured cream	125ml (¼ pint)
Salt	½ × 2.5ml spoon (¼ teaspoon)
Pepper	a good shake
Sugar	a pinch

Method

Add seasonings to yoghurt or soured cream and mix well together.

ADDITIONAL FLAVOURINGS

To the basic recipe any one of the following may be added:-

- Tomato Ketchup
- Chutney
- A few drops soy sauce
- A few drops Worcestershire sauce
- Freshly chopped herbs
- Finely chopped gherkins, capers or olives
- Finely chopped onion
- Crushed or finely chopped garlic cloves
- Small, mashed banana
- Finely chopped nuts
- Honey

Evaporated milk dressing 9

Ingredients

Evaporated milk	1 × 170g (6oz) can
Salt	1 × 2.5ml spoon (½ teaspoon)
Pepper	1 × 2.5ml spoon (½ teaspoon)
Dry mustard	½ × 2.5ml spoon (¼ teaspoon)
Salad oil	6 × 15ml spoons (6 tablesp.)
Lemon juice	2 × 15ml spoons (2 tablesp.)

Evaporated Milk Dressing

The addition of lemon juice thickens the dressing as well as reducing the sweetness of the evaporated milk. This dressing can replace mayonnaise in most salads except in those where the hot vegetables are tossed into the dressing.

Method

1 Place evaporated milk, salt, pepper and mustard in a bowl.

2 Gradually whisk in the oil, then the lemon juice and continue whisking as the dressing thickens.

3 Cover and store in the refrigerator until required (use within 48 hours).

Seafood cocktail dressing 10

Use this dressing with all shell fish salads. Other fish such as sardines, tuna and mackerel can also be mixed with it.

Ingredients

Mayonnaise	125ml (¼ pint) *see page 38*
Tomato ketchup	4 × 15ml spoons (4 tablesp.)
Worcester sauce	a few drops
Lemon juice	1 × 15ml (1 teaspoon)

Method

Mix all ingredients together until they are thoroughly blended into a smooth consistency.

Banana dressing 11

A sweet dressing makes a good accompaniment to salads that have slightly bitter ingredients. Try it with chicory or endive salad for a good contrast of flavours.

Ingredients

Orange	1 small
Banana	1 small
Sugar	1 × 10ml (2 level teaspoons)
Salt	½ × 2.5ml spoon (¼ teaspoon)
Pepper	a good shake
Salad oil	2 × 15ml spoons (2 tablesp.)

Method

1 Cut orange in half and squeeze the juice into a basin.

2 Peel and roughly slice the banana into orange juice. Mash the banana with a fork or pestle until smooth.

3 Add sugar, salt and pepper.

4 Gradually beat in the oil and pour the dressing into a small sauce boat. Serve the dressing separately, allowing each person to moisten his own portion of salad.

Tomato dressing

12

Tomato Dressing
A cool and refreshing dressing that goes well with all green salads and bean sprout salads. It's a good way of using up the over-ripe tomatoes, too.

●
Ingredients

Tomatoes	4 medium-sized soft
Garlic	1 clove
Basil or Parsley freshly chopped	1 × 10ml spoon (2 teaspoons)
Salt	1 × 5ml spoon (1 teaspoon)
Pepper	½ × 2.5ml spoon (¼ teaspoon)
Salad oil	4 × 15ml spoons (4 tablesp.)
Wine vinegar	2 × 15ml spoons (2 tablesp.)

Method

1 Wipe and cut the tomatoes into quarters.
2 Peel, chop and crush the garlic clove with a round-bladed knife or pestle.
3 Place tomatoes and garlic in a liquidiser for about 30 seconds until ingredients are well-blended.
4 Rub the contents of the liquidiser through a sieve until only the pips and skin remain to be discarded.
5 Return the tomato juice to the liquidiser with herbs, salt and pepper and a little oil. Run the machine and slowly add the remaining oil through the top.
6 Add vinegar, then pour the dressing into a bowl and chill in refrigerator

HOW TO MAKE TOMATO PUREE WITHOUT A LIQUIDISER

13

If you don't have a liquidiser, place the tomatoes in boiling water for 1 minute, remove and peel while still hot. Roughly cut the tomatoes and rub them through a sieve to make a thin purée. Add seasonings and slowly whisk-in the oil, then the vinegar.

Rub the tomatoes through the sieve with the back of a wooden spoon.

Coconut dressing 14

An unusual dressing that's good with any salad containing fruit or sweet vegetables.

Ingredients

Coconut desiccated	6 × 15ml spoons (6 tablespoons)
Milk	6 × 15ml spoons (6 tablesp.)
Soured cream	125ml (¼ pint)
Salt	½ × 2.5ml spoon (¼ teaspoon)
Pepper	½ × 2.5ml spoon (¼ teaspoon)
Ground nutmeg	½ × 2.5ml spoon (¼ teaspoon)
Lemon juice	1 × 15ml spoon (1 tablespoon)

Method

1 Mix the coconut and milk together in a bowl. Leave for a few minutes until most of the milk has been absorbed.

2 Add remaining ingredients to the bowl and mix well.

Cheese & onion dressing 15

This dressing is suitable for a wide range of salads. For a milder flavour, try using chives instead of onions.

Ingredients

Onion	1 small
Cream cheese	75g (3oz)
Olive oil	125ml (¼ pint)
Lemon juice	1 × 15ml spoon (1 tablespoon)
Salt	½ × 2.5ml spoon (¼ teaspoon)
Black pepper	freshly ground

Method

1 Peel and rub the onion against the fine holes of a grater to extract the juice.

2 Place the onion juice and cheese in a bowl and mash together until smooth and creamy.

3 Add the oil drop by drop, beating well between each addition. A small balloon whisk is ideal for this. When one-third of the oil has been absorbed, then the rest may be added a little more quickly.

4 Beat in lemon juice, salt and plenty of black pepper.

Garlic dressing 16

This dressing is suitable for most vegetable and bean salads. It is best used within 48 hours of mixing.

●

Ingredients	
Fresh garlic	2 large cloves
Salt	1 × 2.5ml spoon (½ teaspoon)
Salad oil	125ml (¼ pint)
Wine vinegar	2 × 10ml spoons (2 dessertsp.)

●
Method

1 Peel and roughly chop the garlic. Place salt and garlic in a small basin or mortar.

2 Crush the garlic against salt with a pestle until garlic forms a smooth paste.

3 Add oil, drop by drop, beating between each addition. Oil may be added more quickly once the first third has been absorbed.

4 Slacken dressing with the vinegar, beating it in drop by drop.

Peanut dressing 17

Children will not need much persuasion to eat their salads if you coat them in this dressing. Make it just before using.

●

Ingredients	
Peanut butter	2 × 15ml spoons (2 tablesp.)
Pepper	½ × 2.5ml spoon (¼ teaspoon)
Salad oil	5 × 15ml spoons (5 tablesp.)
Lemon juice	2 × 15ml spoons (2 tablesp.)

●
Method

1 Place the peanut butter and pepper in a bowl.

2 Gradually add oil, beating well between each addition.

3 Gradually add sufficient lemon juice to make a coating consistency. Use at once.

ORANGE DRESSING 18

Ingredients	
Juice	from half an orange
Salad oil	2 × 15ml spoons (2 tablesp.)
Wine vinegar	1 × 15ml spoon (1 tablespoon)
Salt	1 × 2.5ml spoon (½ teaspoon)
Pepper	a good shake

Method

Place all ingredients in a bowl and whisk until well blended. Be careful not to overdo the seasoning.

STARTER SALADS

A starter should be a small portion of food served to whet the appetite, not to spoil it for the main course. A salad makes an ideal start to any meal and can be simply one or two fresh vegetables served in an appetising manner. Arrange the salad in individual dishes or, alternatively, on a large serving plate, paying special attention to garnishes *(see page 32)*.

Les crudités

Les Crudités

Crudités are a selection of raw vegetables, either finely grated and served in individual piles on a plate or cut into Julienne strips and served with a well-flavoured dressing. The dressing makes them easy to serve as starters, or with cocktails, because the vegetables are picked up with the fingers and dipped into the sauce.

●

Dressing

Use a Mayonnaise, Soured Cream or Yoghurt Dressing well flavoured with tomato ketchup, Worcestershire Sauce, curry paste, garlic, onion or herbs, etc. *(see page 39/40)*. Serve the dressing in a small bowl.

●

Vegetables

Use a variety of those shown opposite and when prepared, place in ice-cold water to crispen. Serve either in small heaps round the dressing or stand the Julienne strips upright in a small bowl.

●

Serving

If you are serving crudités with a dip dressing, serve each person with a selection on a dish, or leave them in individual piles on separate dishes. This kind of dressing may provide a good excuse for providing your guests with finger bowls.

How to make les crudités

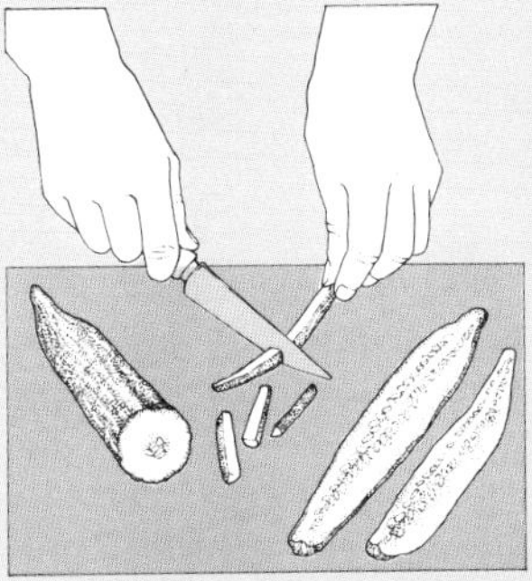

Cucumber/courgette
Wipe, cut into quarters lengthwise and remove seeds. Cut each quarter into 2 or 3 strips, and then into 7cm (3in) lengths.

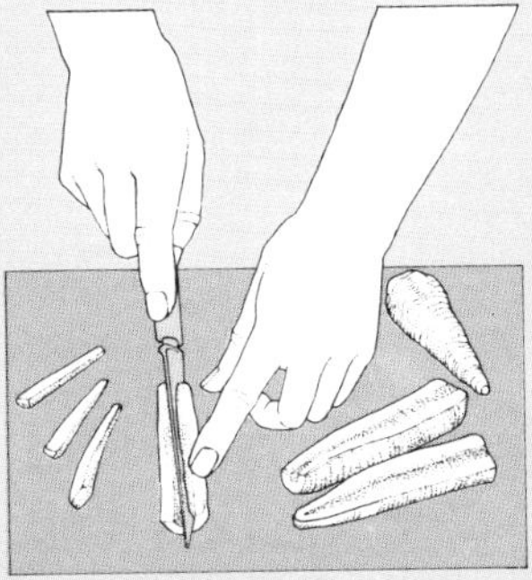

Carrot/parsnip
Trim and scrub. Cut into ½cm (¼in) thick slices. Place two slices together and cut into ½cm (¼in) strips.

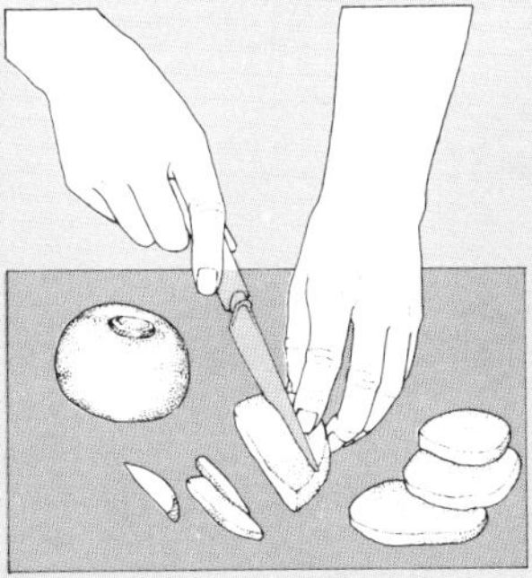

Celeriac/turnip
Peel and cut into ½cm (¼in) thick slices. Place 2 or 3 slices together and cut into ½cm (¼in) wide strips.

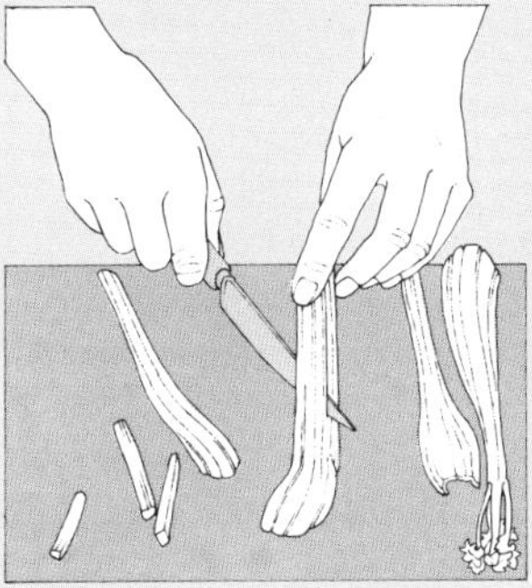

Celery
Scrub stalks and cut into strips down length. Cut each strip into 7cm (3in) lengths.

Radishes
Trim roots and cut off the stalks to within 1cm (½in) of the radish. Wipe clean with a damp cloth.

Salad onions
Trim the roots and the ends of the stalks. Peel off the outer layer of skin and wipe with a damp cloth.

Cucumber minted bowl 1

Cucumber makes a cool, refreshing starter to a meal. This salad is excellent with highly spiced dishes.

Ingredients

Cucumber	1 medium-sized
Natural yoghurt	125ml (¼ pint)
Mint freshly chopped	4 × 10ml spoons (2 rounded dessertspoons)
Salt	1 × 2.5ml spoon (½ teaspoon)
Pepper	½ × 2.5ml spoon (¼ teaspoon)
Sugar	½ × 2.5ml spoon (¼ teaspoon)

Garnish with a few small mint leaves

Method

1. Wipe and thinly slice cucumber. Spread the slices in a colander and leave to drain for 30 minutes.
2. Place yoghurt in a bowl and stir in the remaining ingredients. Leave 30 minutes.

To serve

Pat cucumber slices dry on kitchen paper. Divide the slices between 4 or 6 individual bowls and pour over the yoghurt dressing. Garnish with mint leaves and serve chilled.

Tomato & celery cup 2

Choose large, firm tomatoes for stuffing and serve them well-chilled. If you prefer a milder cheese, use Stilton or a mild crumbly cheese.

Ingredients

Tomatoes	4 large, firm
Celery	5 sticks with leaves
Blue cheese	75g (3oz)
Salt/pepper	to taste
Mayonnaise, or soured cream	2 × 15ml spoons (2 tablespoons)

Method

1. Wipe tomatoes, cut a slice from the top of each and carefully scoop out the centres with a teaspoon. Leave the tomatoes upside down to drain on kitchen paper for 30 minutes.
2. Clean celery and make several cuts from base to centre of four sticks. Leave to curl in ice-cold water *(see page 33)*. Finely chop the remaining stick by cutting into 3 or 4 lengthwise and then thinly slicing across.
3. Finely chop or crumble cheese into a bowl. Add the chopped celery and 1 tablespoon of chopped tomato centre (the remainder could be used to make Tomato Dressing *(see page 43)*.

4. Gently fold mayonnaise or soured cream into the cheese mixture. Season the inside of tomatoes with salt and pepper and fill with cheese mixture. Place tomatoes in refrigerator to chill.

SERVING SUGGESTION FOR TOMATO & CELERY CUPS

Place a tomato on each of 4 individual serving plates with a curled celery stick. Serve them well chilled.

Mushroom & caper salad

A piquant salad that makes an excellent starter to a meal.

Ingredients	
Garlic	2 cloves
Lemon juice	from 1 small lemon
Salt	½ × 2.5ml spoon (¼ teaspoon)
Pepper	a good shake
Water	1 × 15ml spoon (1 tablespoon)
Vinegar	1 × 10ml spoon (1 dessert-spoon) from jar of capers
Mushrooms	250g (½lb) cap or button
Capers	2 × 10ml spoons (2 dessertsp.)
Red pepper	half of a small one

Method

1. Peel and crush garlic cloves and place them with lemon juice, salt, pepper, water and vinegar in a saucepan.
2. Wipe the mushrooms, add to pan and simmer for 3 minutes.
3. Place mushrooms, juice, capers and sugar in a bowl. Leave until cold.
4. Wipe and finely chop the pepper. Add to the salad just before serving.

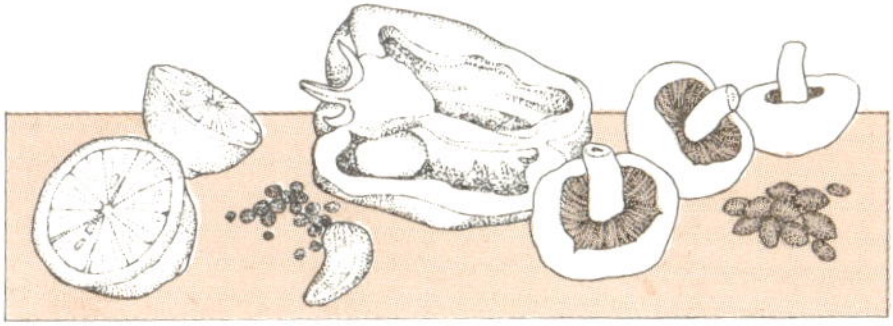

Prawn cocktail

4

with seafood cocktail dressing

Created by the Americans, this cocktail has now become a universally popular starter. Chinese leaves stay crisper than lettuce leaves, but whatever you use, don't add the dressing until just before serving.

●

Dressing ingredients

Mayonnaise	125ml (¼ pint) *see page 38*
Tomato ketchup	4 × 15ml spoons (4 tablesp.)
Worcester sauce	a few drops
Lemon juice	1 × 5ml spoon (1 teaspoon)

●

Salad ingredients

Fresh prawns	300g (¾lb) unpeeled
Chinese leaves or crisp lettuce	

Garnish with lemon wedges and parsley sprigs

●

Method

1. **Dressing.** Make mayonnaise as instructed and stir in the remaining dressing ingredients.
2. **Salad.** Reserve 4 prawns for garnish and peel the remainder.
3. Place half the dressing in a bowl and fold in peeled prawns.

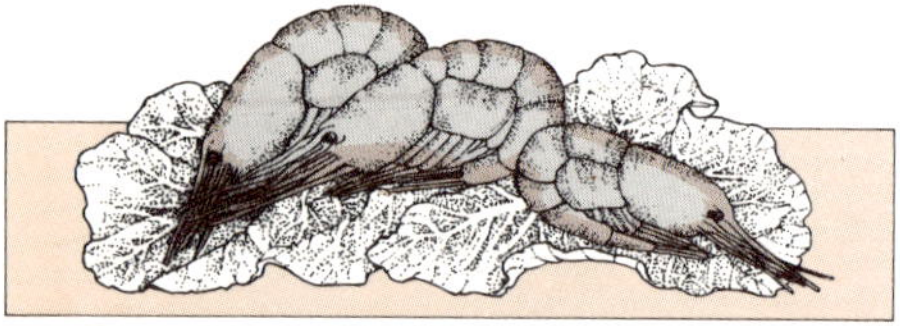

HOW TO SERVE PRAWN COCKTAIL

●

Just before serving, finely shred lettuce or Chinese leaves and three-quarters fill 4 large wine glasses with it.

●

Divide the prawn mixture between the glasses and pour the remaining dressing onto it.

●

Place a small sprig of parsley in the centre of each. Arrange a prawn and a lemon wedge on the rim of each glass *(see page 32).*

Pear & crab starter 5

with cream mayonnaise dressing

Good quality canned pears may be used when fresh pears are unavailable. Fresh pears, however, are preferable because, although they should be ripe and sweet, they will be less syrupy than canned pears.

●

Salad ingredients

Pears	2 large, ripe
Lemon juice	*see method*
Crab meat	1 × 43g (1½oz) can

●

Dressing ingredients

Single cream	*see method*
Mayonnaise	125ml (¼ pint) *see page 38*

Garnish: 4 small tomatoes, salad cress

Method

1. **Salad.** Remove stalks and cut pears in half lengthwise. Remove the skins, carefully scoop out cores and coat pears immediately in lemon juice to prevent discolouration.
2. Divide crab meat between the pear centres then place them, cut side downwards, on four small serving plates.
3. **Dressing.** Fold 2 or 3 tablespoons of cream into the mayonnaise to make a thick coating consistency. Gently pour the dressing over the pears to coat.
4. **Garnish.** Cut tomatoes into waterlily shapes *(see page 32)*. Garnish each plate with tomato and cress.

Chicory & cherry platter 6

with olive oil and lemon juice dressing

The sweetness of cherries contrasts well with the flavour of chicory.

●

Salad ingredients

Chicory	3 medium-sized chicons
Radishes	8 large
Black cherries	1 × 425g (15oz) can

●

Dressing ingredients

Olive oil	2 × 15ml spoons (2 tablesp.)
Lemon juice	1 × 15ml spoon (1 tablesp.)
Salt and pepper	a good shake

●

Method

1. **Salad.** Wipe the chicons and slice them thickly.
2. Wash and thinly slice the radishes.
3. Drain cherries and place them in a bowl with the chicory and radishes.
4. **Dressing.** Place oil, lemon juice and a good shake of salt and pepper into a bottle with a screw-top. Shake the bottle vigorously until the contents are well blended.
5. Pour the dressing over the salad and toss lightly. Serve at once.

Avocado boats

with olive oil and lemon juice dressing

This not only makes a good start to a meal, but served as two halves to each person, it also makes an excellent light lunch. Avocados are the basis for several classic starters; this method of serving them is suitable for the beginning of almost any meal.

●

Dressing ingredients	
Olive oil	2 × 15ml spoons (2 tablesp.)
Lemon juice	1 × 15ml spoon (1 tablespoon)
Salt	1 × 2.5ml spoon (½ teaspoon)
Pepper	½ × 2.5ml spoon (¼ teaspoon)
Sugar	½ × 2.5ml spoon (¼ teaspoon)
Black pepper	freshly ground

●

Salad ingredients	
Tomatoes	4 small, firm ripe
Cheese	75g (3oz) Mozzarella or Edam
Avocado pears	2 large ripe

●

Method

1. **Dressing.** Place all dressing ingredients in a bottle with a screw-top. Shake bottle vigorously until contents are well blended.
2. **Salad.** Remove skins from the tomatoes, either by placing in boiling water for 30 seconds or by placing on a fork and turning in a naked flame until the skins split. Peel while still hot.
3. Finely chop tomatoes and cheese. Place them in a bowl and pour onto the dressing.
4. Cut round avocados lengthwise, twist each into two halves and discard the stones.
5. Carefully scoop out flesh with a teaspoon. Roughly chop flesh, add to bowl and toss ingredients lightly.

HOW TO SERVE AVOCADO BOATS

Place one or two lettuce leaves on 4 individual plates with an empty avocado shell on top.
Pile salad into the shells, placing any extra salad on the lettuce.
Garnish each with a lemon wedge and serve at once.

Avocado & orange salad

Here's a delightful salad that is subtle both in colour and flavour. Serve immediately it is made.

Ingredients

Orange	1 large
Avocado pear	1 large, ripe
Olive oil	4 × 15ml spoons (4 tablesp.)
Lemon juice	1 × 5ml spoon (1 teaspoon)
Salt and pepper	*see method*
Chicory	2 large, or 3 small, chicons
Lettuce leaves or watercress	

Garnish with paprika

Method

1. Hold the orange over a bowl and cut off peel and white pith with a small sharp or serrated knife. Cut down between each segment to remove flesh. Reserve flesh for garnish and juice for dressing.
2. Cut round the avocado lengthwise, twist the two halves apart and discard the stone.
3. Scoop out flesh from one half with a teaspoon and place in a bowl with the orange juice. Mash the avocado until smooth.
4. Slowly beat in oil, then the lemon juice and finally a little salt and pepper.
5. Scoop out the flesh from the second half of the avocado, roughly chop flesh and toss in the dressing to coat.
6. Wipe and thickly slice the chicons, add to bowl and toss lightly.

N.B. *Don't use an over-ripe avocado or the dressing will quickly become discoloured.*

HOW TO SERVE AVOCADO & ORANGE SALAD

Line a shallow serving dish with lettuce or watercress. Pile avocado mixture in centre, garnish with reserved orange and a little paprika. Serve at once.

SIDE SALADS

Most simple salads make good accompaniments to the main dish, especially if the food is spicy or well-flavoured. Serve the salad in individual bowls so that it can be kept separate from the hot food. Make sure the vegetables are cut into manageable pieces because most people prefer to eat the side salad with only a fork, taking small portions alternately with the hot food.

Tomato salad 1

with French dressing

Use firm, ripe tomatoes for this salad and serve it well chilled.

●

Salad ingredients	
Salad tomatoes	½kg (1 lb)
Salad onions	a small bunch
Salt	to taste
Black pepper	freshly ground

●

Dressing ingredients	
Olive oil	2 × 15ml spoons (2 tablesp.)
Vinegar (mint or wine)	1 × 15ml spoon (1 tablespoon)
Salt and pepper	a good shake

●

Method

1. **Salad.** Wipe tomatoes or remove skins *(see page 52)*. Finely slice tomatoes.
2. Peel and finely chop onions, and finely snip stalks for garnish.
3. Layer tomatoes and chopped onions in a shallow dish with plenty of salt and pepper. Sprinkle the stalks on top.
4. **Dressing.** Place all dressing ingredients in a bottle with a screw-top and shake the bottle vigorously until the contents are well blended. Pour over the salad.
5. Cover the dish and leave at least one hour in the refrigerator before serving.

Watercress & orange salad 2
with oil and lemon juice dressing

A light, piquant salad that makes a good accompaniment to serve with a risotto or pasta dish.

●
Salad ingredients

Watercress	2 bunches
Oranges	2 medium-sized
Celery	4 sticks
Stoned dates	112g (4oz)

●
Dressing ingredients

Salad oil	3 × 15ml spoons (3 tablesp.)
Lemon juice	2 × 15ml spoons (2 tablesp.)
Salt and pepper	a good shake

●
Method

1. **Salad.** Remove yellow leaves and the thick stalks from watercress. Wash the watercress and shake dry in a salad basket.
2. Hold the oranges over a serving bowl and cut off peel and white pith with a small sharp or serrated knife. Cut between each segment to release flesh. Place in a bowl.
3. Wash and thinly slice celery.
4. Roughly chop dates and add to bowl
5. **Dressing.** Place all dressing ingredients in a bottle with a screw-top and shake the bottle vigorously until the contents are well blended. Pour the dressing over salad.
6. Break watercress into small sprigs and toss lightly into the salad. Serve at once.

Spinach & caper salad 3
with caper dressing

Spinach makes an excellent substitute when lettuce is expensive.

●
Salad ingredients

Young spinach	250g (½lb)
Tomatoes	250g (½lb)
Onion	1 small

●
Dressing ingredients

Salad oil	2 × 15ml spoons (2 tablesp.)
Wine vinegar	1 × 15ml spoon (1 tablespoon)
Salt	½ × 2.5ml spoon (¼ teaspoon)
Dry mustard	½ × 2.5ml spoon (¼ teaspoon)
Sugar	1 × 2.5ml spoon (½ teaspoon)
Vinegar from caper jar	1 × 5ml spoon (1 teaspoon)
Black pepper	freshly ground
Capers	2 × 10ml spoons (2 dessertsp.)

●
Method

1. Pull fleshy part of spinach leaves from stalks. Wash, and shake dry.
2. Pull the spinach into bite-sized pieces and place in a salad bowl.
3. Wipe and thinly slice tomatoes.
4. Peel and thinly slice onion. Separate rings and add to bowl with the tomatoes.
5. **Dressing.** Place all dressing ingredients, except capers, in a bottle with a screw top. Shake until well blended.
6. Chop capers and add to dressing.

Minted beetroot bowl

with yoghurt and mint dressing

4

Raw beetroot makes a refreshing crunchy salad that's delicious with cold meats. But do serve it in individual bowls to prevent the beetroot discolouring the other foods on the plate.

Dressing ingredients	
Natural yoghurt	125ml (¼ pint)
Chopped mint	2 × 15ml spoons (2 tablesp.)
Demerara sugar	1 × 15ml spoon (1 tablespoon)
Lemon juice	1 × 15ml spoon (1 tablespoon)
Salt and pepper	a good shake

Salad ingredients	
Salad onions	a small bunch
Dessert apple	1 large, green skinned
Beetroot	1 large, uncooked – 250g (10oz)
Sultanas	4 × 10ml spoons (4 dessertsp.)

Garnish ingredients
Lettuce or watercress
Freshly chopped mint
4 lemon wedges

Method

1. **Dressing.** Reserve 1 x 15 ml spoon (1 tablespoon) of yoghurt for garnish and place the remainder in a deep-sided bowl with the other dressing ingredients. Mix well.
2. **Salad.** Peel and finely chop onions.
3. Wipe the apple, cut into quarters and remove the core. Finely chop the apple, add to bowl and toss lightly in the dressing.
4. Peel and coarsely grate the beetroot. Add to bowl with sultanas and toss lightly.
5. Cover the bowl and chill the salad one hour before serving.

HOW TO SERVE MINTED BEETROOT BOWL

Line 4 individual bowls with lettuce or watercress. Divide beetroot salad between them.
Drizzle a little reserved yoghurt over each. Sprinkle with chopped mint and garnish with a wedge of lemon.
Serve at once.

Broad bean & caraway bowl 5

with vinaigrette dressing

This is a delicious way to serve tender new season broad beans.

Salad ingredients

Broad beans	½kg (1 lb) shelled
Onion	1 small
Caraway seeds	2 × 5ml spoons (2 teaspoons)

Dressing ingredients

Olive oil	2 × 15ml spoons (2 tablesp.)
Wine vinegar	1 × 15ml (1 tablespoon)
Sugar	½ × 2.5ml spoon (¼ teaspoon)
Salt	½ × 2.5ml spoon (¼ teaspoon)
Pepper	a good shake
Dry mustard	a pinch

Garnish with croutons (see page 33)

Method

1. **Salad.** Cook beans in boiling, salted water until just tender. Drain the beans and place in a serving bowl.
2. Peel and thinly slice the onion. Separate into rings and add to the bowl with caraway seeds.
3. **Dressing.** Place all dressing ingredients in a bottle with a screw-top and shake the bottle vigorously until the contents are well blended.
4. Pour dressing over beans and mix well until they are coated. Leave salad to cool, turning beans over occasionally.
5. Add croûtons just before serving.

Courgette & tomato salad 6

Baby courgettes can be used raw in salads, but they have more flavour if cooked for a minute or two first.

Ingredients

Courgettes	½kg (1 lb)
Olive oil	3 × 15ml spoons (3 tablesp.)
Rosemary freshly chopped	2 × 5ml spoons (2 teaspoons)
Salt	1 × 2.5ml spoon (½ teaspoon)
Dry mustard	a pinch
Lemon juice	2 × 15ml spoons (2 tablesp.)
Tomatoes	4 medium-sized, firm
Black pepper	freshly ground

Garnish with croutons (see page 33)

Method

1. Wipe and trim both ends of the courgettes. Cut into 1 cm (½ in) slices.
2. Heat the oil in a saucepan. Add the courgettes, cover, and cook for 2 minutes over a low heat. The courgettes should still be crisp.
3. Stir the rosemary, salt, mustard and lemon juice into pan.
4. Wipe and roughly chop the tomatoes. Place the tomatoes and contents of the saucepan into a serving dish. Sprinkle over the salad plenty of black pepper and leave it to cool. Serve chilled with croûtons sprinkled over the salad.

Endive & citrus fruit salad
with banana dressing

Endive is often scarce, so when you do see it in the greengrocers it is well worth buying. There are two types of endive: A curly variety and a broad-leaved which looks very like lettuce.

Salad ingredients	
Endive	1 small
Grapefruit	1 large
Oranges	2 standard
Banana	1 small
Walnuts	50g (2oz) shelled

Dressing ingredients	
Banana	1 small
Sugar	1 × 10ml spoon (1 dessertsp.)
Salt	½ × 2.5ml spoon (¼ teaspoon)
Pepper	a good shake
Salad oil	2 × 15ml spoons (2 tablesp.)

Method

1. Discard any damaged leaves and trim off the base of the endive. Separate into stalks, wash them in cold water and shake dry in a salad basket.
2. Hold the grapefruit over a bowl to collect the juice and cut off the peel and pith with a small sharp, serrated knife. Cut down between the segments to remove flesh.
3. Prepare the oranges in the same way.
4. Break the endive into manageable pieces and place in a salad bowl.
5. Peel and thinly slice the banana and toss in the fruit juice to coat. Remove banana with a draining spoon and add to the salad bowl with grapefruit, oranges and walnuts.

HOW TO MAKE BANANA DRESSING

Peel and roughly slice banana, place them in a bowl with fruit juice and mash with a fork or pestle until smooth.
Add the sugar, salt and pepper.
Gradually beat in oil and pour the dressing into a small sauce boat. Serve separately, allowing each person to moisten his own portion of salad.

Sweet pepper & tomato salad
with garlic dressing

This colourful salad will compliment most main courses. Use a vinaigrette dressing if a milder dressing is preferred.

Salad ingredients

Red pepper	1 large
Green pepper	1 large
Tomatoes	½kg (1 lb) ripe
Onion	1 medium sized
Black olives	12
Salt	*see method*
Black pepper	freshly ground

Dressing ingredients

Garlic	2 large fresh cloves
Salt	1 × 2.5ml spoon (½ teaspoon)
Salad oil	125ml (¼ pint)
Wine vinegar	2 × 10ml spoons (2 dessertsp.)

Method

1. **Salad.** Place peppers under a moderately hot grill, turning them frequently until the skins are well charred. Remove the skins while still hot.
2. Cut each pepper in half lengthwise, remove stalks, seeds and white pith. Cut the peppers into thin strips.
3. Place the tomatoes in boiling water for 30 seconds. Remove skins and thickly slice the tomatoes.
4. Peel and thinly slice the onion and then separate into rings.
5. Layer peppers, tomatoes, onion and olives in a bowl with plenty of salt and pepper.

DRESSING/GARNISHING/SERVING
Make Garlic Dressing as instructed on page 45. Pour dressing over salad, toss ingredients lightly and leave at least 30 minutes before serving. Freshly chopped chervil may be sprinkled over salad if you wish.

Potato & fennel salad

with cream mayonnaise or yoghurt dressing

If using left-over vegetables for this salad, the fennel may be added raw to the dressing.

●

Dressing ingredients

Cream mayonnaise	125ml (¼ pint)
Top of the milk	2 × 15ml spoons (2 tablesp.)
or	
Yoghurt dressing	125ml (¼ pint) *(see page 41)*

●

Salad ingredients

Waxy potatoes	½kg (1 lb)
Carrots	250g (½ lb)
Fennel root	1 small
Chopped parsley	2 × 10ml spoons (2 dessertsp.)
Salt	1 × 2.5ml spoon (½ teaspoon)
Black pepper	freshly ground

Garnish with freshly chopped parsley or fennel

●

Method

1 **Dressing.** Stir milk into mayonnaise or make Yoghurt Dressing in a large bowl.

2 **Salad.** Scrub the potatoes and cook them in boiling water for 10 to 15 minutes until just cooked but still firm. Remove the skins while still hot.

3 Scrub the carrots, trim both ends and cut them into 2 or 3 pieces, if they are large.

4 Wipe the fennel root, cut in half lengthwise and thickly slice across width. Reserve any leaves for the garnish.

5 Cook carrots and fennel in a little salted water until the carrots are just tender. Drain immediately.

6 Roughly chop the potatoes and carrots, and fold carefully into the dressing with the fennel, parsley, salt and plenty of black pepper.

7 Serve the salad hot or chilled, garnished with chopped parsley or a few fennel leaves.

USING POTATOES IN SALADS

To avoid loss of nutrients when cooking potatoes, cook them in their jackets.While the potato is hot the skins will rub off easily. If you are using left-over potatoes, cool them quickly, or add them to the dressing while still hot.

Red cabbage & gherkin slaw 10

with mayonnaise or vinaigrette dressing

Use either Vinaigrette Dressing or Mayonnaise for this salad, but remember the red cabbage will bleed and discolour the mayonnaise.

●

Dressings (use either)	
Mayonnaise	125ml (¼ pint) *see page 38*
Vinaigrette	8 × 15ml spoons (8 tablespoons) *see page 38*

●

Salad ingredients	
Red cabbage	250g (8oz)
Celeriac	250g (8oz)
Onion	1 medium sized
Dessert apples	2 medium sized
Gherkins	8 large

●

Method

1 **Dressing.** Make the preferred dressing, and place in a large bowl.

2 **Salad.** Trim and finely shred cabbage *(see page 21)* and toss into the dressing.

3 Peel and coarsely grate the celeriac, add to the bowl and toss the ingredients.

4 Peel and finely chop the onion.

5 Wipe and cut apples into quarters. Remove the cores, coarsely grate the apples and add to the bowl with the onions.

6 Thickly slice gherkins and add to the salad. Prepare at least an hour before serving.

Cole slaw 11

with mayonnaise dressing

The secret of a good cole slaw is to shred the cabbage finely. If large quantities are made, an electric or manual shredder is useful.

●

Dressing	
Mayonnaise	125ml (¼ pint) *see page 38*

●

Salad ingredients	
White cabbage	200g (8oz)
Onion	1 medium sized
Carrots	2 medium sized
Celery	4 to 6 sticks
Sultanas	75g (3oz)

●

Method

1 **Dressing.** Make the dressing as instructed.

2 **Salad.** Trim and finely shred the cabbage, roughly chop and place in a large bowl *(see page 21)*.

3 Peel and thinly slice the onion.

4 Wash and coarsely grate the carrots.

5 Wash and thinly slice the celery.

6 Place onion, carrots, celery and sultanas into the bowl.

7 Add dressing and fold into the salad until all ingredients are well coated. Leave the salad at least 30 minutes before serving.

Jerusalem artichoke & cucumber salad

with soured cream dressing

Jerusalem artichokes are small, knobbly tubers in season from October to March. They can be added to most cooked vegetable salads, but to enjoy their subtle flavour to the full, try serving them with cucumber or orange in a Soured Cream Dressing.

Dressing ingredients

Soured cream	125ml (¼ pint)
Salt	1 × 2.5ml spoon (½ teaspoon)
Pepper	½ × 2.5ml spoon (¼ teaspoon)
Sugar	½ × 2.5ml spoon (¼ teaspoon)
Dry mustard	½ × 2.5ml spoon (¼ teaspoon)
Chopped herbs	3 × 15ml spoons (3 tablesp.)
Lemon juice	1 × 15ml spoon (1 tablespoon)

Salad ingredients

Jerusalem artichokes	½kg (1 lb)
White vinegar	4 × 15ml spoons (4 tablesp.)
Cucumber	10cm (4in) piece
Almonds	25g (1oz) toasted

Garnish with watercress, paprika and cucumber twists (see page 32)

Method

1. **Dressing.** Place the soured cream in a large bowl, add remaining dressing ingredients and mix well.
2. **Salad.** Scrub the artichokes, place in a saucepan with the vinegar (to prevent discolouration) and cover with cold water. Bring to the boil and cook for 4 minutes. Remove small artichokes and cook the remaining ones a further 2 to 3 minutes.
3. Scrape off as much skin as possible while still hot, avoiding cutting away too much artichoke. Cut them into bite-sized pieces and toss immediately into dressing. Place the salad in refrigerator to chill.
4. Wipe and cut cucumber into quarters lengthwise. Cut each piece into 1.5cm (½in) slices and toss into salad with ¾ of the almonds.

HOW TO SERVE JERUSALEM ARTICHOKE & CUCUMBER SALAD

Place the salad in a serving bowl, arrange watercress round the edge and garnish the salad with a good shake of paprika, cucumber twists and the remaining almonds.

Cauliflower & Brussels sprout bowl

with oil and vinegar dressing

Brussel sprouts make a good, inexpensive salad during the winter months, while cauliflower florets give a good 'bite' to the salad.

Dressing ingredients

Salad oil	6 × 15ml spoons (6 tablesp.)
Wine vinegar	2 × 15ml spoons (2 tablesp.)
Salt	½ × 2.5ml spoon (¼ teaspoon)
Pepper	½ × 2.5ml spoon (¼ teaspoon)
Sugar	½ × 2.5ml spoon (¼ teaspoon)
Mustard (made)	2 × 5ml spoons (teaspoons)

Salad ingredients

Cauliflower	1 small, firm
Radishes	1 bunch
Mushrooms	100g (4oz) button type
Brussels sprouts	250g (8oz) small, firm

Method

1 **Dressing** Place all dressing ingredients in a bottle with a screw top and shake the bottle vigorously until the ingredients are well blended. Pour the dressing into a large bowl.

2 Trim base and green leaves from cauliflower, and break into small florets (use thick stalk and leaves as a vegetable). Place the cauliflower in cold water for a few minutes, drain well and then toss into the dressing. Leave at least 30 minutes.

3 Trim, wash and thickly slice the radishes.

4 Wipe the mushrooms and leave them whole unless they are too large. Toss the radishes and mushrooms into the dressing.

HOW TO SERVE CAULIFLOWER & BRUSSEL SPROUT BOWL

Trim base and outer leaves from Brussel sprouts. Shred sprouts finely across width, separate into strips and toss lightly into dressing.

Serve salad immediately in individual bowls.

Alternatively, use a Tomato Dressing *(see page 43)* or Garlic Dressing *(see page 45)*.

MAIN MEAL SALADS

The salads on the following pages are substantial enough to be served as main dishes, although many of them could be served as accompaniments to other dishes.

Main course salads

Salads as the main course need not be restricted to hot summer days. Whenever a light meal or packed lunch is needed, you'll find a variety of suitable vegetables throughout the year. A good plate of salad vegetables can stand on its own, but is even better if served with a selection of cheeses or cold meats and you'll find most supermarkets now have a wide selection of these. Serve the salad with fresh brown bread, pitta bread, crispbread or small boiled potatoes tossed in melted butter and freshly chopped herbs.

Chicory, prune & ham salad 1

Prunes cooked this way will keep several days in the refrigerator, making a delicious addition to salads.

●

Ingredients	
Dried prunes	24
Cider vinegar	7 × 15ml spoons (7 tablesp.)
Sugar	50g (2oz)
Lettuce leaves	6 to 8
Chicory	2 large chicons
Radishes	12 large
Ham	8 thin slices

●

Method

1. Place prunes and vinegar in a small saucepan with sufficient water to just cover them and bring slowly to the boil.
2. Remove pan from heat and leave the prunes to soak for at least 3 hours (or overnight if possible).
3. Add sugar, bring slowly to the boil, then simmer for 5 to 10 minutes until the prunes are soft but still whole. Leave in the pan until cold.
4. Wash and shake lettuce dry in a salad basket.
5. Wipe and thinly slice the chicons and radishes.
6. Cut the ham into thin ribbons.

HOW TO SERVE CHICORY, PRUNE & HAM SALAD

●

Finely shred the lettuce and divide between 4 individual bowls or small plates.

●

Arrange the ham in a ring round edge of lettuce. Remove prunes from liquor with a draining spoon and place in the centre of bowls with radishes and chicory.

●

Pour a little prune liquor over salads and serve immediately.

Celery & grapefruit salad

with honey and yoghurt dressing

2

The sweet dressing used here blends well with most vegetables, but is especially good with those that have a slightly bitter or earthy flavour.

●

Dressing ingredients

Natural yoghurt	125ml (¼ pint)
Honey	2 × 10ml spoons (2 dessertsp.)
Salt	½ × 2.5ml spoon (¼ teaspoon)
Lemon juice	1 × 5ml (1 teaspoon)

●

Salad ingredients

Chinese leaves	250g (½lb)
Celery	6 sticks with leaves
Cap mushrooms	50g (2oz)
Cooked meat	200g (7oz)
Carrots	2 large
Grapefruit	1 large

●

Method

1. **Dressing.** Mix all dressing ingredients together in a large bowl.
2. **Salad.** Thinly slice, wash and drain the Chinese leaves.
3. Clean celery, remove leaves and reserve for garnish. Cut the celery into thin slices.
4. Wipe and thinly slice the mushrooms.
5. Roughly chop the meat.
6. Scrub and coarsely grate the carrots.
7. Place the Chinese leaves, celery, mushrooms, meat and two-thirds of the carrot into the dressing and toss the ingredients lightly to coat. Place the salad in a serving bowl.
8. Hold the grapefruit over a bowl and cut off the peel and white pith with a small sharp or serrated knife. Cut down between each segment to remove the flesh.
9. Arrange the grapefruit down the centre of the salad. Toss the remaining carrot in the grapefruit juice and place down either side of the grapefruit.
10. Garnish the salad with reserved celery leaves. Serve at once.

●

Tip *If you wish, the salad can be made in advance omitting the Chinese leaves. Toss in at the last moment.*

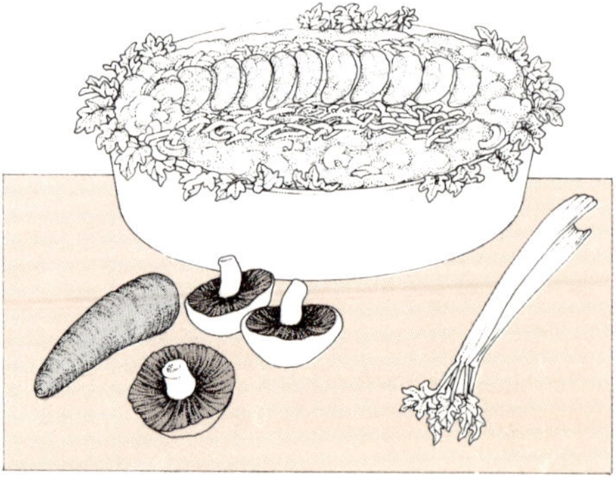

Carrot & date salad

with cheese and onion dressing

3

This salad keeps well so it is a good one to make for packed lunches.

Dressing ingredients

Onion	1 small
Cream cheese	75g (3oz)
Olive oil	125ml (¼ pint)
Lemon juice	1 × 15ml spoon (1 tablespoon)
Salt	½ × 2.5ml spoon (¼ teaspoon)
Black pepper	freshly ground

Salad ingredients

Carrots	250g (8oz)
Dessert apples	2 large, green skinned
Stoned dates	100g (4oz)
Eggs	4 – 6 hard boiled
Watercress or lettuce	

Method

1. **Dressing.** Make Cheese and Onion Dressing as instructed on page 44.

2. **Salad.** Scrub and coarsely grate the carrots. Toss each carrot into the dressing as it is grated.

3. Wipe the apples, cut into quarters and remove cores. Roughly chop the apples and toss them in with the carrots.

4. Roughly chop the dates and add them to the salad. Cover the bowl and leave for several hours before serving.

HOW TO SERVE CARROT & DATE SALAD

Remove the shells and cut the eggs into quarters lengthwise. Line a serving bowl with watercress or lettuce and pile the carrot salad in centre. Arrange 6 egg quarters on top and serve the remainder separately.

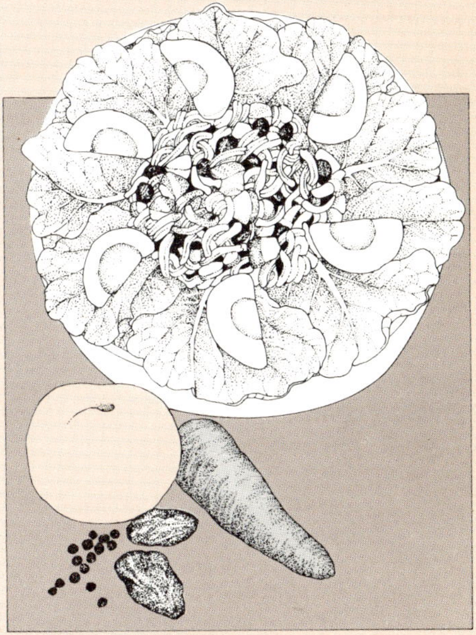

Pickled beet salad 4

with oil and vinegar dressing

Stilton cheese and beetroot are excellent companions. Here is a quickly prepared salad to prove it.

●

Salad ingredients	
Salad onions	1 bunch
Stilton cheese	180g (6oz)
Walnuts	25g (1oz) shelled
Pickled beet	1 × 500g (1¼lb) bottle
Dressing ingredients	
Salad oil	2 × 15ml spoons (2 tablesp.)
Vinegar from beet bottle	2 × 15ml spoons (2 tablespoons)
Chopped mint	2 × 15ml spoons (2 tablesp.)

Method

1. Peel onions and reserve the smallest ones for garnish. Roughly chop the remainder, including stalks.
2. Cut the cheese into small cubes.
3. Roughly chop the walnuts.
4. Remove beets with a draining spoon and place them in a bowl with the onions, cheese and walnuts. Larger beets can be halved if necessary.
5. Place all the dressing ingredients in a bottle with a screw top and shake the bottle vigorously until the ingredients are well blended.
6. Pour the dressing over the salad and mix lightly together. Cover and leave for at least 30 minutes.

Chicken & sesame seed salad 5

with soy sauce dressing

This is a delicious way to serve the left-over meat from a Sunday roast.

●

Garnish ingredients	
Salad oil	1 × 10ml spoon (1 dessertsp.)
Egg	1 standard

●

Dressing ingredients	
Lemon juice	1 × 15ml spoon (1 tablespoon)
Salad oil	2 × 15ml spoons (2 tablesp.)
Soy sauce	2 × 15ml spoons (2 tablesp.)
Demerara sugar	2 × 10ml spoons (2 dessertsp.)
Sesame seeds roasted	4 × 10ml spoons (4 dessertspoons)

●

Salad ingredients	
Cooked chicken	300g (12oz)
Tomatoes	250g (8oz)
Cucumber	7cm (3in) piece

Method

1. **Garnish.** Heat the oil in a small omelet plan. Beat the egg, pour into the pan and cook over a low heat until set but not browned. Slide the omelet onto a plate and roll up tightly. Leave to cool.
2. **Dressing.** Place all dressing ingredients in a bowl and mix well together.
3. **Salad.** Cut the chicken into small pieces and fold into the dressing to coat. Place the meat in the centre of a serving plate.

4. Wipe the tomatoes and cucumber, slice thinly and arrange them alternately round the edge of the plate.
5. Cut the omelet into thin slices and place over the meat to garnish.

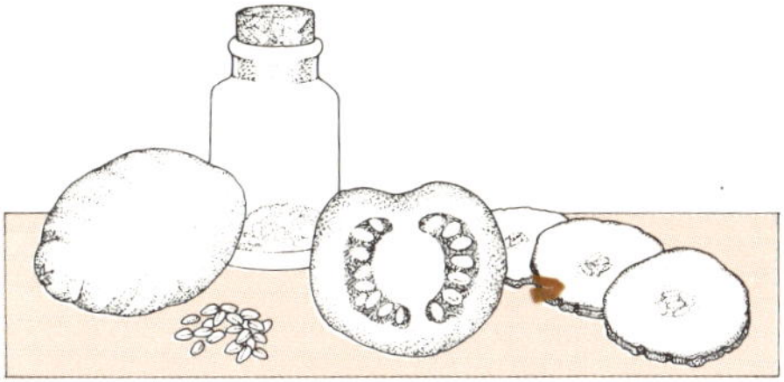

HOW TO SERVE CONTINENTAL BEAN SALAD
Roughly chop the hard-boiled egg and place in the centre of salad. Cut each salami slice to the centre and fold over to form a cone. Arrange the salami cones radiating out from the egg, and place a small sprig of parsley between each one.

Alternatively: *If dried beans are used and cooked, try the salad with Garlic Dressing (see page 45) or a mild French Dressing (see page 37).*

Continental bean salad

6

Here's a substantial salad that makes use of the liquor from the cans of beans and corn for the dressing.

●

Salad ingredients	
Red kidney beans	1 × 213g (7½oz) can
Butter beans	1 × 213g (7½oz) can
Sweet corn	1 × 326g (11½oz) can
Continental sausage	250g (½lb)
Onion	1 small
Green olives	12 stuffed

Dressing ingredients	
Mustard	1 x 15ml spoon (1 tablespoon)
Olive oil	1 x 15ml spoon (1 tablespoon)
Liquor from can of beans	125ml (¼ pint)

Garnish with hard boiled eggs, slices of salami and sprigs of parsley

Method

1. **Salad.** Drain the contents from cans of beans and corn and place them in a bowl. Reserve liquors for dressing.
2. Slice the sausage and add to the bowl.
3. Peel and thinly slice the onion, separate into rings and add to the bowl.
4. Slice the olives and place in the bowl.
5. **Dressing.** Measure liquors and make up to 125ml (¼ pint) with water if necessary.
6. Blend mustard and oil together. Slowly beat in liquor.
7. Pour the dressing over the salad and toss well to mix.

Rice salad
with French dressing

Rice makes a good base for a salad. Any left-over cooked root or stalk vegetables may be added as well as cooked meat or fish.

●

Salad ingredients

Long grain rice	150g (6oz)
Celery	4 sticks
Red peppers	2 medium sized
Gherkins	12 cocktail size
Sweet corn	1 × 198g (7oz) can
Peanuts	100g (4 oz) salted
Black olives	12 large
Pineapple	1 × 227 g (8oz) can of pieces

●

Dressing ingredients

Salad oil	3 × 15ml spoons (3 tablesp.)
Wine vinegar	2 × 15ml spoons (2 tablesp.)
Pepper	½ × 2.5ml spoon (¼ teaspoon)
Salt	*see method*

●

Method

1. Cook the rice in boiling, salted water until just tender. Drain well, then spread the rice over a large plate to dry.
2. Wash and finely chop the celery.
3. Wipe the peppers and cut in halves lengthwise. Discard stalks, seeds and white pith and finely chop the peppers.
4. Cut 6 gherkins into fans (*see page 32*) and reserve. Roughly chop the remainder.
5. Place the cold rice in a large bowl and lightly mix with a fork to separate grains.
6. Add celery, peppers, chopped gherkins, contents of the can of corn, peanuts and olives to the bowl.
7. Drain syrup from the can of pineapple and reserve. Roughly chop the pineapple, if necessary, and add to the bowl.
8. Lightly toss the ingredients together with a fork.
9. Place oil, vinegar, 3 tablespoons of pineapple juice, pepper and a little salt in a bowl. Whisk until the ingredients are well blended. Pour the dressing over the salad and toss lightly to mix.
10. Garnish with reserved gherkin fans and serve with cold meats or fish.

Sprouted seeds & pasta salad
with oil and lemon juice dressing

You'll need to start growing your salad seeds 4 to 5 days in advance of making this salad. Alternatively, use salad cress from the greengrocer.

Dressing ingredients

Lemon juice	from 1 lemon
Salad oil	2 × 15ml spoons (2 tablesp.)
Salt	½ × 2.5ml spoon (¼ teaspoon)
Pepper	½ × 2.5ml spoon (¼ teaspoon)

Salad ingredients

Sprouted seeds	100g (4oz) *see page 29*
Avocado pear	1 large
Tomatoes	4 – 5 medium sized
Pasta shells	100g (4oz) cooked
Cheese or continental sausage	150g (6oz)

Method

1. **Dressing.** Place all dressing ingredients in a bottle with a screw-top and shake the bottle vigorously until the contents are well blended. Pour dressing into a large bowl.
2. **Salad.** Place sprouted seeds in a sieve and rinse under gently running cold water. Separate the shoots and leave to drain.
3. Cut round the avocado lengthwise, gently twist to separate into two halves and discard the stone. Scoop out the flesh with a small teaspoon or melon ball scoop and toss immediately into the dressing to coat.
4. Wipe and roughly chop tomatoes. Add to the bowl with pasta shells.
5. Roughly chop the cheese or Continental sausage, add to salad and toss all the ingredients lightly together.

HOW TO SERVE SPROUTED SEED & PASTA SALAD

Just before serving, add half the sprouted seeds to the salad, lightly toss and place in a serving bowl. Arrange the remaining sprouted seeds round salad to garnish.

Egg & vegetable hives

Any seasonal vegetables may be finely grated or chopped for this salad.

Egg hives ingredients

Eggs	6 hard boiled
Parmesan cheese	50g (2oz) grated
Mayonnaise	125ml (¼ pint) *see page 38*
Single cream or milk	

Salad ingredients

Celeriac	250g (8oz)
Vinaigrette	8 × 15ml spoons (8 tablespoons) *see page 38*
Carrots	4 small
Red pepper	1 small
Baby beets	6 cooked
Tomatoes	8 small, firm
Cucumber	18cm (7in) piece

Method

1. **Eggs.** Shell eggs and cut into halves lengthwise. Scoop out the yolks, place in a basin with the cheese and mash until smooth. Moisten with a little mayonnaise and spread the mixture thickly over the cut surfaces of eggs. Place eggs on a plate, cut side downwards.
2. Beat sufficient cream or milk into the mayonnaise to make a thick, coating consistency. Place a little mayonnaise on top of the egg halves, allowing it to fall and coat the eggs smoothly.
3. **Salad.** Peel and finely grate the celeriac and toss in a little dressing to coat.
4. Trim, wash and finely grate carrots. Toss in a little dressing to coat.
5. Peel pepper *(see page 29)*, cut in half lengthwise and discard stalk, seeds and white pith. Cut twelve thin strips, then finely chop remainder.
6. Peel and finely chop beets.
7. Wipe and roughly chop tomatoes.
8. Wipe and cut 4 thick slices from cucumber. Cut the remainder into Julienne strips *(see page 32)*. Remove centres from round slices and insert cucumber strips through the rings.
9. **To Serve.** With a palette knife, carefully lift up the eggs and place round a large serving plate or in 4 individual plates.
10. Arrange small heaps of the vegetables (except pepper strips) round the plate and set the cucumber bundles in the centre. Pour the remaining dressing over vegetables.
11. Place a strip of pepper diagonally over each egg.

Tomato & bean sprout salad

with tomato dressing

Serve this salad with plenty of fresh wholewheat bread to 'mop' up the delicious juices.

●

Salad ingredients

Bean shoots	350g (12oz)
Green pepper	1 medium sized
Tomatoes	4 medium sized
Salad onions	1 bunch
Cooked meat	350g (12oz)

●

Dressing ingredients

Tomatoes	4 medium sized, soft
Garlic	1 clove
Basil or Parsley freshly chopped	2 × 5ml spoons (2 teaspoons)
Salt	1 × 5ml spoon (1 teaspoon)
Pepper	½ × 2.5ml spoon (¼ teaspoon)
Salad oil	4 × 15ml spoons (4 tablesp.)
Wine vinegar	2 × 15ml spoons (2 tablesp.)

Garnish with 2 hard boiled eggs and 8 black olives

●

Method

1. **Salad.** Rinse bean shoots in cold water and drain well.
2. Wipe the pepper and cut in half lengthwise. Remove stalk, seeds and white pith and roughly chop the pepper.
3. Wipe and roughly chop the tomatoes.
4. Peel and chop the onions, including stalks.
5. Place prepared vegetables in a serving bowl.
6. Roughly chop the meat and two-thirds of the vegetables. Reserve remainder for garnish.
7. **Dressing** Make the Tomato Dressing as instructed on *page 43* and pour over the salad.
8. Place the salad in the refrigerator for at least one hour.

HOW TO SERVE TOMATO & BEAN SHOOT SALAD

Place the reserved meat in the centre of salad. Cut eggs into quarters lengthwise and arrange them round the edge of the meat radiating towards the edge of the salad. Place an olive between each egg quarter.

Chicken salad

with cream and mayonnaise dressing

This salad stays crisp so it is ideal for packed lunches or a buffet party.

Salad ingredients

Red pepper	1 medium sized
Split almonds	25g (1oz)
Celery	6 to 8 sticks
Sultanas	75g (3oz)
Cooked chicken	300g(12oz)
Radishes	1 bunch
Cucumber	7.5cm (3in) piece

Dressing ingredients

Single cream	2 × 15ml spoons (2 tablesp.)
Mayonnaise	125ml (¼ pint) *see page 38*

Method

1. Place the pepper under a moderately hot grill, turning frequently until the skin is well charred. Remove the skin while still hot.
2. Cut the pepper in half lengthwise and remove stalk, seeds and white pith. Cut the pepper into thin strips.
3. Toast the almonds under the grill.
4. Clean and finely slice the celery. Place in a bowl with the sultanas.
5. Roughly chop the chicken.
6. Wash and thinly slice the radishes and place them in a separate bowl with the chicken.

DRESSING AND SERVING CHICKEN SALAD

Stir cream into the mayonnaise and mix half into the chicken mixture and the remainder into the celery mixture.

Place the celery mixture round edge of a serving dish with the chicken mixture in the centre.

Wipe and finely slice the cucumber. Arrange the cucumber round the edge of the dish and pepper strips radiating out from the centre. Sprinkle nuts on top.

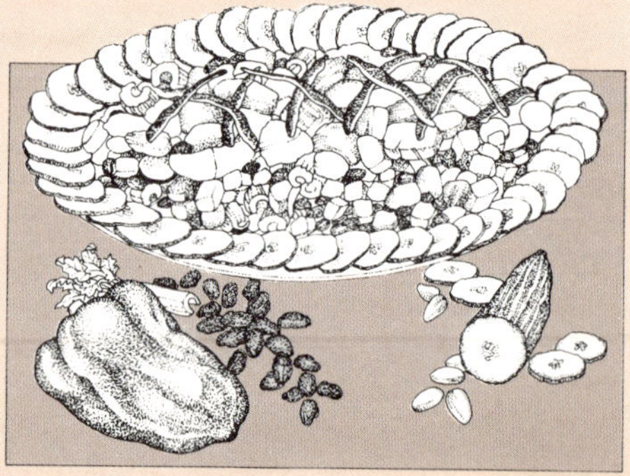

Oriental fish salad

White fish is very good in salads if served raw and very fresh, as in Japan, or quickly cooked in a piquant sauce as in this salad. Choose firm, thick cuts of fish for the best result.

Ingredients

White fish	½kg (1 lb) must be firm
Tomatoes	750g (1½lb)
Olive oil	4 × 15ml spoons (4 tablesp.)
Soy sauce	1 × 5ml spoon (1 teaspoon)
Salt and pepper	*see method*
Green pepper	1 medium sized
Fennel root	1 small
Cap mushrooms	100g (4oz)
Bean shoots	250g (8oz)
Prawns	100g (4oz) shelled

Method

1. Cut fish into 2.5cm (1in) cubes, discarding bones and skin.
2. Wipe and roughly chop the tomatoes.
3. Heat oil, soy sauce and a good shake of salt and pepper in a pan. Add the fish and half the tomatoes and cook over a low heat for 2 to 3 minutes until the fish is cooked but still firm. Remove from heat and leave to cool.
4. Wipe the pepper, cut in half lengthwise and remove stalk, seeds and white pith. Roughly chop the pepper.
5. Wipe the fennel and cut in half lengthwise. Cut each half into thin slices across width.
6. Wipe and thinly slice the mushrooms.
7. Place the pepper, fennel and mushrooms in a serving bowl.
8. Rinse the bean shoots in cold water and drain well. Add to the bowl.
9. Remove the fish with a draining spoon and add to the bowl with the prawns.
10. Rub the contents of saucepan through a sieve and pour the juice over the salad.
11. Toss the salad lightly and serve at once.

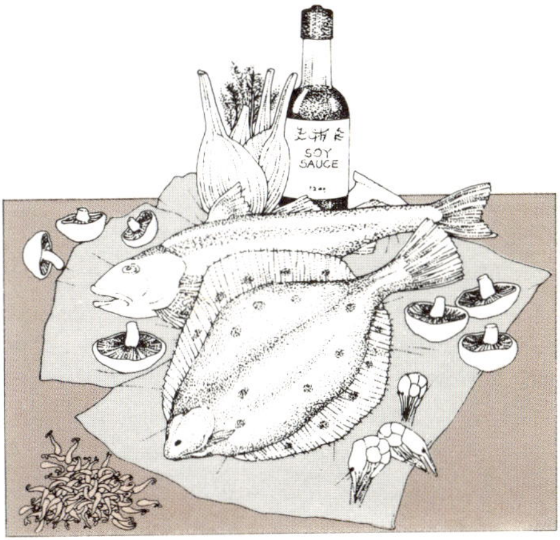

Apple & celeriac salad

with coconut dressing

A refreshing, crunchy salad with an unusual coconut dressing.

●

Dressing ingredients

Desiccated coconut	6 × 15ml spoons (6 tablespoons)
Milk	6 × 15ml spoons (6 tablesp.)
Soured cream	125ml (¼ pint)
Salt	½ × 2.5ml spoon (¼ teaspoon)
Pepper	½ × 2.5ml spoon (¼ teaspoon)
Ground nutmeg	½ × 2.5ml spoon (¼ teaspoon)
Lemon juice	1 × 15ml spoon (1 tablespoon)

●

Salad ingredients

Celeriac	250g (8oz)
Dessert apples	1 red skinned, 1 green skinned
Chicory	1 medium sized chicon
Black grapes	125g (4oz)
Ham	4 – 6 slices

●

Method

1. **Dressing.** Mix the coconut and milk together in a large bowl. Leave for a few minutes, then add the remaining dressing ingredients and mix well.

2. **Salad.** Peel and finely chop the celeriac, add to dressing and mix well together.

3. Wipe and cut the apples into quarters. Remove cores, finely chop the apples and fold them into the dressing.

4. Thinly slice the chicons and fold them into the dressing.

5. Wipe and cut the grapes into halves. Remove pips and fold the grapes into the dressing, reserving a few for garnishing.

HOW TO SERVE APPLE & CELERIAC SALAD

Place the salad on a serving dish with the reserved grapes in the centre. Cut ham slices into halves, roll up loosely and arrange round the salad.

Fruit & nut salad
with yoghurt dressing

14

A refreshing, crunchy salad to serve with any cold meat, hard-boiled eggs or a variety of cheeses.

Dressing ingredients

Natural, or nut flavoured yoghurt	125ml (1/4 pint)
Salt and pepper	a good shake

Salad ingredients

Hazel nuts	50g (2oz) shelled
Oranges	2 medium sized
Dessert apples	2 red skinned
Celery	4 sticks
Black olives	12
Watercress	1 bunch

Method

1. **Dressing.** Place all dressing ingredients in a large bowl and mix well.
2. **Salad.** Place the hazelnuts under a moderately hot grill until evenly toasted.
3. Hold the oranges over the bowl of dressing and cut off peel and white pith with a small sharp or serrated knife. Cut down between each segment to release the flesh. Cut the segments in half and add to dressing.
4. Wipe the apples, cut into quarters and remove cores. Finely chop the apples and toss immediately into the dressing.
5. Clean and finely slice the celery. Add to the bowl with olives and nuts.
6. **To serve** Remove yellow leaves and thick stalks from the watercress. Wash and shake the watercress, dry in a salad basket, break sprigs into manageable pieces and place in a serving bowl.
7. Pile the salad in the centre and garnish with a small sprig of watercress.

Red bean bounty 15

For a substantial vegetarian dish, replace the bacon with nuts of your choice.

Salad ingredients

Streaky bacon	6 rashers
Onion	1 medium sized
Salad oil	3 × 15ml spoons (3 tablesp.)
Wine vinegar	2 × 15ml spoons (2 tablesp.)
Salt and pepper	*see method*
Kidney beans	1 × 265g (10oz) can – red type
Herbs freshly chopped	2 × 10ml spoons (2 dessertspoons)
Lettuce, endive or watercress	

Garnish with lemon wedges

Method

1. Remove rind and roughly chop bacon.
2. Place the bacon in a saucepan and cook over a low heat until the fat runs.
3. Peel and thinly slice the onion. Add the oil and onion to pan, cover, and cook over a moderate heat for 2 minutes.
4. Remove from heat and stir in vinegar or lemon juice and a good shake of salt and pepper.
5. Drain the liquid from the can of beans. Add beans and herbs to the saucepan and toss ingredients lightly to coat. Leave salad to cool.
6. Line 2 or 3 individual bowls with lettuce, endive or watercress, and divide the salad between the bowls.

Tomato & cheese salad 16

with French dressing

It is well worth buying goats' cheese and the large continental tomatoes for this salad if you wish to recapture the atmosphere of those splendid Greek islands.

●

Salad ingredients

Onion	1 small
Tomatoes	2 medium sized
Salt	*see method*
Hard goats cheese (or blue)	75g (3oz)
Black olives	6 to 8

●

Dressing ingredients

Olive oil	2 × 15ml spoons (2 tablesp.)
Wine vinegar	1 × 15ml spoon (1 tablespoon)
Salt	½ × 2.5ml spoon (¼ teaspoon)
Black pepper	freshly ground

●

Method

1. Peel and thinly slice the onion. Separate into rings and arrange half on an individual serving plate.
2. Wipe and roughly chop the tomatoes. Place over the onions, sprinkle liberally with salt and cover with remaining onion rings.
3. Roughly dice cheese and sprinkle over salad with the olives.

DRESSING FOR TOMATO AND CHEESE SALAD

Place all dressing ingredients in a bottle with a screw top and shake the bottle vigorously until the contents are well blended. Pour half the dressing over the salad and serve with plenty of freshly ground black pepper and chunks of wholewheat bread.

DRESSING FOR SALAMI PLATTER

Place all dressing ingredients in a bottle with a screw top and shake the bottle vigorously until the contents are well blended.
Drizzle some of the dressing over the salad.
Serve with plenty of freshly ground black pepper.

Salami platter

with French dressing

17

A Continental salad is often arranged by placing small heaps of each ingredient on a plate, instead of tossing them altogether.

●

Salad ingredients	
Tomato	1 medium sized
Carrot	1 small
Onion	1 small
Gherkins	4
Salami	4 – 6 slices

●

Dressing ingredients	
Olive oil	2 × 15ml spoons (2 tablesp.)
Wine vinegar	1 × 15ml spoon (1 tablespoon)
Salt and pepper	a good shake

●

Method

1. **Salad.** Wipe and thinly slice tomato.
2. Scrub and finely grate the carrot.
3. Peel and finely chop the onion.
4. Thickly slice 3 gherkins. Cut the remaining one into a fan *(see page 32)*.
5. Arrange the salami, tomatoes, carrot and onion in heaps round an individual plate. Place the sliced gherkins in centre and gherkin fan on salami.

HOT SALADS

There is no reason to suppose that a salad is, by definition, cold. Many hot dishes which are composed of vegetables may reasonably be described as salads. These pages offer a few suggestions for using easily available vegetables in hot dishes.

Preparation

Most vegetables are suitable for hot salads but leafy kinds such as lettuce, watercress and spinach are best not cooked. Chinese leaves, if tossed into the hot salad just before serving, will retain some of their crispness if the stalk end is used.

To serve hot
Choose salads that have mainly cooked vegetables in them and toss the freshly cooked vegetables immediately into the dressing. Serve at once.

Heated salads
Salads are best eaten within a few hours of preparation but left-over salads containing suitable raw vegetables can be heated. Heat about 1 × 15ml spoon (1 tablespoon) oil in a pan, toss in the salad and cover. Heat for 2 to 3 minutes only, turning the salad over once or twice. Turn the salad immediately into a serving dish and serve at once. If you own a microwave oven, then simply cover the salad bowl with cling film and heat for 1 to 2 minutes.

Important
Don't over-heat the salad as this will cause the vegetables to lose their crispness and the dressing to separate. The salads in this section can be served either hot or cold.

Ratatouille salad

A delicious mixture of vegetables served either hot or cold.

Salad ingredients

Aubergine	1 medium sized
Courgettes	250g (8oz)
Tomatoes	500g (1¼lb)
Red pepper	1 medium sized
Green pepper	1 medium sized
Onion	1 large
Salt	*see method*

Dressing ingredients

Olive oil	5 × 15ml spoons (5 tablesp.)
Wine vinegar	2 × 15ml spoons (2 tablesp.)
Salt	*see method*
Black pepper	freshly ground

Method

1. Wipe aubergine, courgettes, tomatoes and peppers with a damp cloth.
2. Cut the aubergine into thick slices and layer them in a colander with a little salt.
3. Cut courgettes into 1cm (½in) slices.
4. Thickly slice the tomatoes.
5. Cut the peppers into halves lengthwise and remove stalks, seeds and white pith. Cut the peppers into thick strips.
6. Peel and thickly slice the onion, then separate into rings.
7. Rinse aubergines thoroughly in cold water and pat the slices dry with kitchen paper.
8. Heat olive oil in a large pan.
9. Add onions and aubergines, cover and cook over a low heat for 2 minutes, shaking the pan once or twice.
10. Add the remaining vegetables, cover and continue cooking for 5 minutes, shaking the pan occasionally or gently turning the vegetables over without breaking them.
11. Remove vegetables with a draining spoon and place in a serving bowl (the onions, peppers and courgettes should still be crisp).
12. Stir vinegar, a little salt and plenty of pepper into the pan. Pour the dressing over the vegetables.
13. Serve salad hot, or well chilled.

N.B. *Quantity of salt required will depend on how well the aubergines were rinsed after salting. This process removes excess water and bitterness from the aubergine.*

Hot kebab salad

with soured cream dressing

Choose any firm, crisp vegetable to thread on long skewers. Remember not to overcook the vegetables or they soften and fall off the skewers.

●

Dressing ingredients

Soured cream	125ml (¼ pint)
Salt	½ × 2.5ml spoon (¼ teaspoon)
Pepper	½ × 2.5ml spoon (¼ teaspoon)
Sugar	½ × 2.5ml spoon (¼ teaspoon)
Dry mustard	½ × 2.5ml spoon (¼ teaspoon)
Chopped herbs	3 × 15ml spoons (3 tablesp.)

●

Salad

Choose 3 or more of the following vegetables and prepare as instructed:-

Cucumber
Wipe and cut into 1cm (½in) thick slices

Courgette
Wipe and cut into 2cm (¾in) thick slices

Mushrooms
Wipe and remove stalks

Small onions
Place in cold water, bring slowly to the boil and cook one minute. Remove and peel while still hot.

Small tomatoes
Wipe.and cut skins round centre of tomatoes

Celeriac
Remove peel and cut celeriac into quarters. Cut into thick slices and use raw, or cook in boiling water for 2 minutes

Celery
Clean stalks and cut into 5cm (2in) long pieces

Green/red pepper
Wipe and cut into quarters lengthwise. Discard stalk, seeds and white pith and cut each quarter into 3 or 4 pieces.

●

Method

1. **Dressing.** Place the soured cream in a bowl, add the remaining dressing ingredients and mix well.
2. **Salad.** Prepare the vegetables as instructed. Thread alternately onto long skewers or kebab sticks and brush vegetables with oil.
3. Preheat a grill on a high mark, place the kebabs on grill rack and cook for 3 to 4 minutes only, turning them frequently and brushing with oil, if required. Vegetables should be hot but still very crisp.
4. Serve the kebabs immediately on a bed of rice or shredded Chinese leaves. Serve the dressing separately.

Mixed root vegetable salad

with cream mayonnaise dressing

Most root vegetables can be served this way, but make sure you choose young, tender roots or you may find them a little woody.

●

Dressing ingredients

Mayonnaise	125ml (¼ pint) *see page 38*
Single cream	2 × 15ml spoons (2 tablesp.)
Salt	½ × 2.5ml spoon (¼ teaspoon)
Pepper	a good shake

●

Salad ingredients

Waxy potatoes	½kg (1 lb)
Parsnips	250g (8oz) young
Celeriac	250g (8oz)
Chopped parsley	2 × 15ml spoons (2 tablesp.)

●

Method

1. **Dressing.** Mix all dressing ingredients together in a large bowl.
2. **Salad.** Scrub the potatoes and cook in boiling, salted water for 10-15 minutes until just tender, but still firm. Remove the skins while still hot.
3. Prepare another pan of boiling, salted water.
4. Scrub and cut parsnips in half lengthwise. Remove the cores and roughly chop the parsnips.
5. Peel and cut the celeriac into 1cm (½in) cubes and place with the parsnips and celeriac in the prepared pan. Return water to the boil and cook for 3 minutes only, then drain the vegetables.
6. Roughly chop the potatoes and fold gently into the dressing with parsnips, celeriac and parsley.
7. Serve the salad hot or cold.

Tip *when cooking vegetables for a salad, toss them in the dressing while they are still hot. They will absorb the flavour of the dressing while they are cooling. Uncooked root vegetables, and others with tough fibres, can be left to marinate in the dressing for some time. This will soften them considerably.*

French bean salad 4

Mangetout and very young runner beans are good served this way, too.

●
Ingredients

French beans	½kg (1 lb)
Bacon	8 rashers
Salad oil	4 × 15ml spoons (4 tablesp.)
Lemon juice	1 × 15ml spoon (1 tablespoon)
Sugar	1 × 5ml spoon (1 teaspoon)
Ground nutmeg	1 × 5ml spoon (1 teaspoon)
Salt	1 × 2.5ml spoon (½ teaspoon)
Lemon wedges	

●
Method

1. Wipe the beans and trim both ends.
2. Remove rind, cut the bacon into small pieces and cook in a saucepan over a low heat until the fat runs.
3. Add the oil and beans, cover and cook for 3 to 4 minutes (beans should still be crisp).
4. Stir the remaining ingredients, except the lemon, into pan.
5. Place the beans and juices into a serving dish.
6. Serve the salad hot or well-chilled, garnished with lemon wedges.

Celeriac & carrot salad 5

with cream mayonnaise dressing

Celeriac has a slightly sweet taste and is milder in flavour than celery.

●
Dressing ingredients

Mayonnaise	6 × 15ml spoons (6 tablesp.)
Single cream	2 × 15ml spoons (2 tablesp.)
Mustard (made)	1 × 5ml spoon (1 teaspoon)

●
Salad ingredients

Carrots	250g (8oz)
Celeriac	1 medium sized

Garnish with freshly chopped parsley

●
Method

1. **Dressing.** Mix all dressing ingredients together in a large bowl.
2. **Salad.** Prepare a pan of boiling salted water.
3. Wash and cut the carrots into thin sticks *(see page 21)*.
4. Peel and cut the celeriac into thin sticks *(see page 24)*.
5. Place the carrots and celeriac into the prepared water, return the water to the boil and cook for 2 minutes only.
6. Drain the vegetables and toss immediately in the dressing. Serve hot or leave the salad to cool. Serve sprinkled with chopped parsley.

N.B. *The quantity of mustard may be varied according to taste.*

MOULDED SALADS

Setting vegetables in a mould is an attractive way to serve a salad, but they should be prepared several hours in advance.

Finely chop or grate the vegetables to make the salad easier to serve, and use only sufficient setting agent to hold the ingredients together. Too firm a set will mar the textures of the vegetables.

Most vegetables, except leafy ones, are suitable to use in a moulded salad.

Melon boats

This makes an attractive salad to serve as a starter to any meal. Alternatively serve as a light, midday snack.

●
Ingredients

Honeydew melon	1 small
Sweetcorn	1 × 198g (7oz) can
Gelatine	2 × 10ml spoons (2 dessertsp.)
Cider vinegar	2 × 15ml spoons (2 tablesp.)
Salt	1 × 2.5m spoon (¼ teasp.)
Sugar	1 × 5ml spoon (1 teaspoon)
Pepper	a good shake
Ham	100g (4oz) thinly sliced

Garnish with salad cress

●
Method

1. Cut the melon in half from stalk to stem. Discard the pips and remove the flesh with a melon scoop or small spoon to make balls. Place the melon balls in a sieve over a basin and leave for 30 minutes.
2. Strain the contents of a can of corn into the sieve with the melon.
3. Place 45ml (3 tablespoons) water in a small measuring jug and sprinkle gelatine onto it. Place the jug in a saucepan of hot water and stir until the gelatine has dissolved.
4. Stir the vinegar, salt, sugar, pepper, melon and corn juice into the gelatine. Make up to 125ml (¼ pint) with water, if necessary.
5. Cut the ham into short thin strips.
6. Place the ham, corn and melon balls alternately into the melon shells.
7. Gently pour over the gelatine mixture and place the shells in the refrigerator until the juice is set. Support the shells over small basins if necessary.

HOW TO SERVE MELON BOATS

Slice each melon half through the centre lengthwise. Garnish the plates with salad cress.

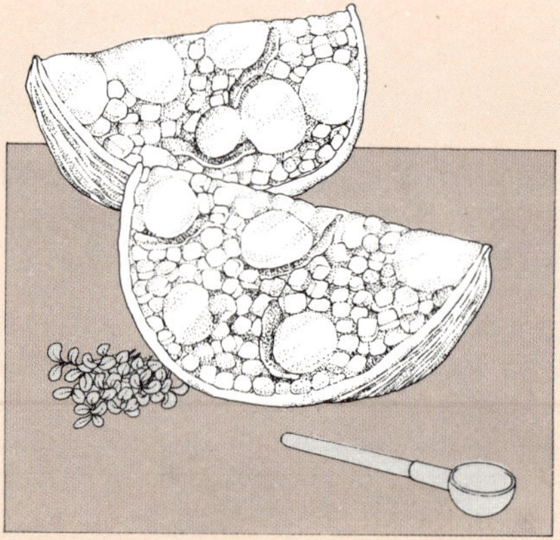

Mixed vegetable mould

The vegetables should be finely chopped for a moulded salad otherwise it is difficult to serve.

Ingredients

Carrots	3 medium sized
Celery	3 sticks
Red pepper	1 medium sized
Onion	1 small
Frozen corn	100g (4oz)
Frozen peas	100g (4oz)
Aspic granules	for 500ml (1 pint) liquid

Garnish with celery leaves or shredded lettuce and onion rings

Method

1. Trim, wash and finely dice the carrots and celery.
2. Wipe and cut the pepper in half lengthwise. Discard the stalk, seeds and white pith and finely chop the pepper.
3. Peel and finely slice the onion. Separate into rings and reserve a few for garnish. Finely chop the remainder.
4. Cook the carrots in a little boiling, salted water for 2 minutes. Add the remaining vegetables including corn and peas. Return the water to the boil and cook for a further 3 to 4 minutes until the vegetables are almost cooked but still crisp.
5. Drain the vegetables and reserve the liquor.
6. Place aspic granules in a measuring jug, add the reserved liquor and sufficient water to make up to 500ml (1 pint) stirring continuously.
7. Place the vegetables in a 1 litre (2 pint) capacity mould or loaf tin. There should be sufficient vegetables to fill the mould.
8. When the aspic liquid is cold, gently pour over the vegetables to the top of mould. Place the mould and any remaining aspic in the refrigerator and leave until set.

HOW TO SERVE MIXED VEGETABLE MOULD

Place mould in hot water for 30 seconds. Cover with a serving plate, invert and carefully remove mould.
Roughly chop remaining aspic. Arrange celery leaves or lettuce round the edge of the plate with aspic on top. Garnish mould with reserved onion rings.

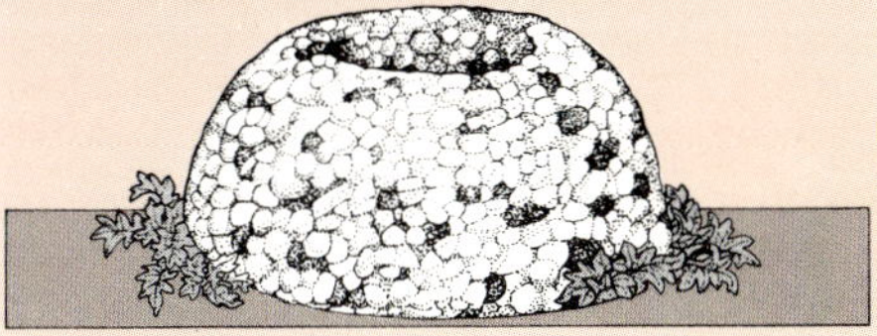

N.B. *Alternatively, replace aspic granules with gelatine and flavour with half a beef extract cube.*

Cucumber & cream cheese mousse

A rich, creamy mousse that can also be served in ramekin dishes.

Ingredients

Cucumber	1 small
Carrots	2 medium sized
Lemon juice	*see method*
Tomatoes	6 medium sized
Red pepper	1 medium sized
Gelatine granules	to set ½ litre (1 pint) liquid
Cream cheese	100g (4oz)
Salt	1 × 2.5ml spoon (½ teasp.)
Pepper	½ × 2.5ml spoon (¼ teasp.)
Mayonnaise	125ml (¼ pint) *see page 38*
Milk	100ml (2½ fl. oz)

Method

1. Wipe the cucumber, remove a 5cm (2in) piece from centre and reserve it for the garnish. Coarsely grate the remaining cucumber, place in a sieve and leave to drain for 30 minutes.
2. Trim, wash and finely grate the carrots. Toss immediately in a little lemon juice.
3. Place the tomatoes in boiling water for 30 seconds, remove and peel them while still hot. Cut the tomatoes into halves. Scoop out the centres and press in a sieve to remove the juice. Reserve the juice and finely chop the tomatoes.
4. Peel the pepper *(see page 29)*. Cut in half lengthwise, discard the stalk, seeds and white pith and finely chop the pepper.
5. Place 4 × 15ml spoons (4 tablespoons) water in a small basin, sprinkle over the gelatine and stand the basin in hot water until the gelatine has dissolved. Remove the basin and leave to cool.
6. Beat the cream cheese, salt and pepper together until smooth, then gradually beat in the mayonnaise.
7. Slowly whisk the tomato juice, milk and gelatine into the mayonnaise mixture and continue whisking until light and foamy.
8. Sprinkle a quarter of the chopped pepper round the base of a wetted 1 litre (2 pint) capacity ring mould.
9. Press the cucumber to remove excess liquid and fold into the mayonnaise with carrots, tomatoes and remaining pepper. Taste and add more seasoning, if necessary.
10. Pour the mixture into a mould and place in the refrigerator until set.

HOW TO SERVE CUCUMBER & CREAM CHEESE MOUSSE

Stand the mould in hot water for 15 seconds, place a serving plate on top, invert and carefully remove mould. Cut reserved cucumber into wheels *(see page 32)* and arrange slices overlapping round edge of plate. Keep the mousse in the refrigerator until ready to serve.

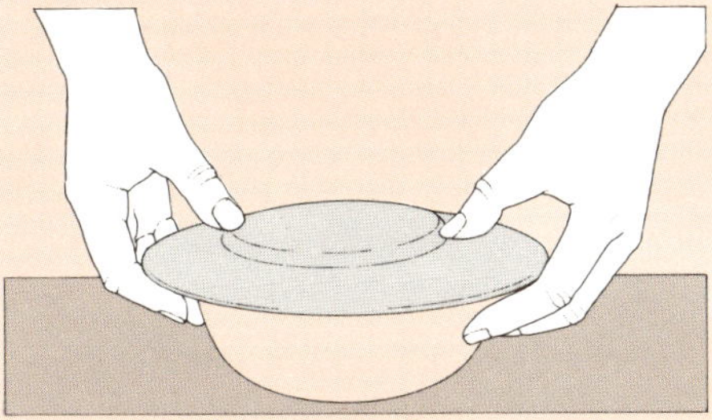

Place serving plate over mould

Invert, and remove mould

Seafood ring

4

Moist rice can be moulded into various shapes, either with wet hands or by packing it into any mould, tin or basin.

●

Ingredients	
Rice	200g (8oz) long grain
Tomatoes	6 medium sized
Green pepper	1 medium sized
Onion	1 small
Chopped parsley	2 × 15ml spoons (2 tablesp.)
Capers	2 × 10ml spoons (2 dessertsp.)
Sweet corn	1 × 198g (7oz) can
Tuna fish	1 × 198g (7oz) can
Lemon juice	1 × 15ml spoon (1 tablesp.)
Salt	1 × 2.5ml spoon (½ teasp.)
Pepper	½ × 2.5ml spoon (¼ teasp.)

Garnish: 100g (4oz) unpeeled prawns, parsley

●

Method

1. Cook the rice in boiling, salted water until just tender. Drain well, then spread it over a plate to cool.
2. Place the tomatoes in boiling water for 30 seconds. Remove from water and peel them while they are still hot. Roughly chop the tomatoes.
3. Wipe and cut the pepper in half lengthwise. Discard the stalk, seeds and white pith. Finely chop the pepper.
4. Peel and finely chop the onion.

Continued overleaf

Seafood ring continued

5. Place the rice in a large bowl and mix lightly with a fork to separate the grains.
6. Add the tomatoes, green pepper, onion, parsley, capers and the contents of a can of corn.
7. Roughly flake the tuna and add to the rice with lemon juice, salt and pepper.
8. Toss the salad lightly with a fork until the ingredients are well mixed.
9. Lightly press the salad into a wetted 1 litre (2 pint) capacity ring mould. Cover, and place in a refrigerator until cold.

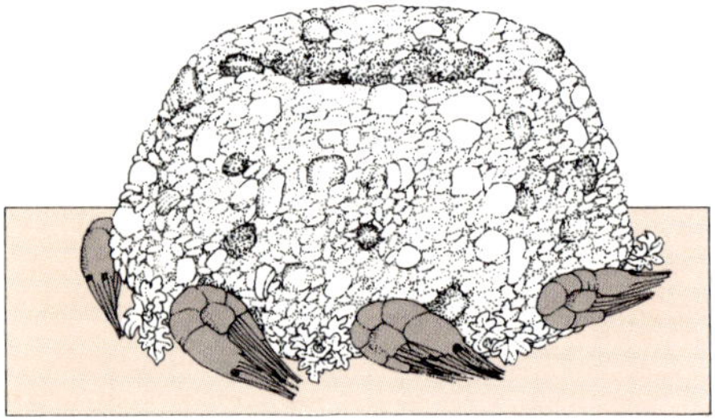

To serve

Loosen the salad round the top of the mould, place a serving plate on top and invert the mould. Shake the mould 2 or 3 times, then carefully remove. Stand prawns round the edge of the mould with a sprig of parsley in between each one.

LIQUID SALADS

Liquid salads are a pleasant way to serve all the nutrients of a fresh salad without the bulk that some elderly people, young children and invalids find difficult to digest. They also make excellent appetisers or refreshing summer drinks.

How to make liquid salads

The vegetables and fruit are simply liquidised together to make a purée. A few suggestions for liquid salads are included in the next few pages, but it's very simple to devise your own using the ingredients you have available.

Points to remember

1 Add only sufficient water to allow the machine to run efficiently, otherwise the salad will be too watery.

2 If you sieve the salad after liquidising, remember to scrape the ingredients from the underside of the sieve from time to time, and use a metal sieve.

3 Add plenty of seasoning and experiment with fresh herbs.

4 You can freeze a liquid salad but remember to leave a 2.5cm (1 in) head space in the container. When thawed the salad may separate, so whisk or place in the liquidiser for a few seconds before serving.

5 15ml (1 tablespoon) salad oil helps to enrich the drink but as this may separate on chilling, always stir a liquid salad before serving.

6 Serve a liquid salad well chilled.

N.B. *The following recipes all make approximately 250ml (½ pint) thick purée to serve like a cold soup. Make up to 375ml (¾ pint) with water if serving as a drink.*

Apple & orange refresher 1

Ingredients	
Orange	1 large
Dessert apples	2 green-skinned
Celery	2 sticks
Lemon juice	2 x 15 ml spoons (2 tablespoons)
Cider vinegar	1 x 10 ml spoons (1 dessertsp.)
Water	2 x 15 ml spoons (2 tablespoons)
Salt	½ x 25 ml spoon (¼ teaspoon)
Sugar	1 x 2.5 ml spoon (½ teaspoon)
Ground nutmeg	½ x 2.5 ml spoon (¼ teaspoon)

Garnish with celery leaves or oranges slices

Method

1. Hold the orange over a plate and cut off the peel and white pith with a small, sharp or serrated knife. Roughly chop the orange, discard the pips, and place in a liquidiser with the juice.

2. Wipe and cut the apple into quarters. Remove the cores and roughly chop the apples.

3. Wash and roughly chop the celery and add to the liquidiser with the apple and the remaining ingredients.

4. Run machine until the contents make a thick purée. Taste, and add more seasoning if necessary. Place the salad in refrigerator to chill.

5. To serve Pour into small bowls or glasses *(see note)* and garnish with celery leaves or orange slices.

Cucumber cool 2

Ingredients	
Cucumber	1 x 7.5cm (3 in) piece
Green pepper	1 small
Dessert apple	1 green-skinned
Water	6 x 15 ml spoons (6 tablespoons)
Lemon juice	1 x 15 ml spoon (1 tablespoon)
Salt	1 x 2.5 ml spoon (½ tablespoon)
Pepper	a good shake

Garnish with cucumber slices or mint leaves

Method

1. Wipe and roughly chop the cucumber.

2. Wipe the pepper and cut in half lengthwise. Discard stalk, seeds and white pith and roughly chop the pepper.

3. Wipe and cut the apple into quarters. Remove the core, roughly chop the apple and place in a liquidiser with the cucumber, pepper and remaining ingredients.

4. Run the machine until the contents make a thick purée. Taste, and add more seasoning if necessary.

5. Place the salad in refrigerator to chill.

6. To serve Pour into small bowls or glasses, *(see note)* garnish with cucumber slices or mint leaves and serve chilled.

Tomato & celery cup

3

Ingredients	
Tomatoes	4 large over-ripe
Celery	4 sticks
Carrot	1 medium-sized
Salad oil	2 x 15 ml spoons (2 tablesp.)
Worcester sauce	1 x 5 ml spoon (1 teaspoon)
Salt	1 x 2.5 ml spoon (½ teaspoon)
Pepper	½ x 2.5 ml spoon (¼ teaspoon)
Sugar	½ x 2.5 ml spoon (¼ teaspoon)
Dry mustard	a pinch

Garnish with celery leaves

Method

1. Wipe and roughly chop the tomatoes.
2. Wash and roughly slice the celery.
3. Wash and chop the carrot.
4. Place the tomatoes, celery, carrot and remaining ingredients in a liquidiser.
5. Run machine until the contents make a thick purée.
6. Rub the contents of the liquidiser through a wire sieve until only the seeds, skin and a few fibres remain.
7. Make the liquid salad up to 250 ml (½ pint) with water, taste and add more seasoning if necessary, place in the refrigerator to chill.
8. **To serve** Pour the chilled salad into 2 or 3 glasses and garnish with celery leaves.

Carrot & celery cup

4

Ingredients	
Carrots	2 medium sized
Celery	3 sticks
Water	5 x 15 ml spoons (5 tablespoons)
Lemon juice	1 x 15 ml spoon (1 tablespoon)
Salt	1 x 2.5 ml spoon (½ teaspoon)
Pepper	a good shake
Dry mustard	a pinch

Garnish with celery leaves

Method

1. Wash and finely chop the carrot.
2. Wash and roughly chop the celery.
3. Place carrots, celery and the remaining ingredients in a liquidiser and run machine until the contents make a thick purée. Taste and add more seasoning, if necessary.
4. Place the salad in refrigerator to chill.
5. **To serve** Pour the salad into small bowls or glasses *(see note)* and garnish each with celery leaves. Serve well chilled.

Index

Figures in italics refer to illustrations

Acknowledgments

The 'How To' Book of Salads and Summer Dishes was created by Simon Jennings and Company Limited. We are grateful to the following individuals and organisations for their assistance in the making of this book:

Lindsay Blow: *all line and tone illustrations*
John Couzins: *cover and title page photographs*
The Dover Archive: *engravings and embellishments*
Ann Hall: *compilation of index*
Peter Higgins: *all food photography*
Jacqui Hine: *preparation of salad dishes*
Marta Jennings: *additional artwork*
Peter Mackertich: *photograph page 17*
Chris Perry: *additional artwork*
A. A. Paul and D. A. T. Southgate: *Food Composition Chart*
Van Withney-Johnson: *photographs pages 6/7*

Typesetting by Text Filmsetters Ltd., Orpington, Kent
Headline setting by Diagraphic Typesetting Ltd., London
Additional display setting by Facet Photosetting, London

Special thanks to Norman Ruffell and the staff of Swaingrove Ltd., Bury St. Edmunds, Suffolk, for the lithographic reproduction.